83

PLANT HARDINESS ZONES

This map, which was developed by the Agricultural Research Service of the U.S. Department of Agriculture, will help you select the most suitable plants for your garden. Every plant included in the "Directory" is given a zone range. The zones 1–11 are based on the average annual minimum temperature. In the zone ranges given, the smaller number indicates the northern-most zone in which a plant can survive the winter and the higher number gives the most southerly area in which it will perform consistently. Bear in mind that factors such as altitude, wind exposure, proximity to water, soil type, snow, night temperature, shade, and the level of water received by a plant may alter a plant's hardiness by as much as two zones.

11

BOLD AND

EXOTIC PLANTS

Using form and shape to create
visual impact in the garden

B O L D AND
EXOTIC PLANTS

NOËL KINGSBURY

with photography by **ANDREA JONES**

WATSON-GUPTILL PUBLICATIONS / NEW YORK

First published in the United Kingdom
in 2000 by Ryland Peters & Small
Cavendish House
51–55 Mortimer Street
London W1N 7TD

First published in the United States in 2000 by
Watson-Guptill Publications,
a division of BPI Communications, Inc.,
1515 Broadway,
New York, NY 10036

Senior Designer Paul Tilby
Senior Editor Sian Parkhouse
Production Meryl Silbert
Head of Design Gabriella Le Grazie
Publishing Director Anne Ryland

Produced by Sung Fung Offset Binding Co. Ltd.
Printed in China.

ISBN 0-8230-0286-1
Library of Congress Card Number: 99-68051

First printing, 2000
1 2 3 4 5 6 7 8 9 / 07 06 05 04 03 02 01 00

page 1 Canna lily hybrid

page 2 *Yucca gloriosa*

page 3 *Vitis coignetiae*

pages 4 and 5 *Melianthus major*

CONTENTS

A GARDEN WITHOUT ANY BOLD OR
EXOTIC PLANTS IS LIKE A GARDEN
WITHOUT ANY COLOR. THESE
PLANTS CREATE IMPACT OVER A
LONG SEASON THROUGH THE
STRENGTH OF THEIR FORM OR
FOLIAGE, AND SO THEY ARE PART
OF THE ESSENTIAL FRAMEWORK OF
THE GARDEN, AS WELL AS
ACTING AS FOCAL POINTS, OR
PUNCTUATION MARKS, HELPING TO
GUIDE THE EYE OF THE VIEWER.

INTRODUCTION

OPPOSITE: The foliage of *Hosta sieboldiana* is echoed by the giant rhubarb, *Gunnera manicata*.

ABOVE: *Vitis coignetiae* is a climber related to the grapevine.

FOLIAGE IN THE GARDEN

Gardening has traditionally been about flowers, with leaves playing very much a supporting role. Yet this varies from place to place and from culture to culture. I remember that when I ran a nursery many years ago, I always had a lot of French customers, perhaps because of my relative proximity to two English Channel ports. After a short while it became very easy to predict the plants they would home in on to buy, which were usually completely different from those that the British customers focused on. Their distinguishing characteristic seemed to be unusual or particularly elegant leaves. It was as if gardeners from two neighboring countries were looking at plants in two completely different ways.

In a surprising number of gardening cultures, flowers do not play a particularly important role. In the classical garden tradition, which originated in Renaissance Italy and still remains very influential in most Latin countries, the formal arrangement of clipped hedges and of evergreen trees and shrubs provides the main element of the composition. In the tropics, too, flowers often play a subsidiary role; I remember visiting Rio de Janeiro and being impressed by so many windowboxes that featured a rich array of exotic foliage plants—there was hardly a flower to be seen.

Gardens that focus too much on flowers can be at a distinct disadvantage. Flowers are relatively short lived and are often rather weather dependent; think of how rain can ruin shrub roses or a very hot dry summer curtail a display of flowering annuals. Leaves are with us a lot longer, all year round in the case of evergreens. It makes sense to make greater use of foliage in the garden to lengthen the season and deepen the pleasure that a garden can bring.

Small gardens are particularly difficult to keep interesting all the time, which makes them an especially important place in which to experiment with foliage. A tiny garden needs plants that really earn their keep, and at the very least always look neat—one messy specimen can let down the whole display. With a skillful combination of foliage plants, it is possible to have a garden that is beautiful all year round in even the most constricted space.

It is no surprise that some of the best small garden designs are inspired by the Japanese garden tradition, with an emphasis on elegant foliage and plant form, often quite sparingly planted. There is a strong tradition in Japan of courtyard planting, for example, where every plant is important and where any imperfection or failing would be immediately noticeable. Choosing a limited number of truly first-rate plants has always been an important part of creating a successful garden on such an intimate scale.

ABOVE FAR LEFT: *Trachycarpus fortunei*, the Chusan palm, is a hardy palm that comes from the mountains of China.

ABOVE LEFT: Invaluable for rapidly screening or covering walls, *Aristolochia macrophylla* (Dutchman's pipe) is a vigorous climber.

FAR LEFT: *Blechnum chilense* is a moisture-loving fern that makes wonderfully Jurassic-looking groundcover in mild climates.

LEFT: *Ficus carica*, the fig, is often underrated as a bold foliage plant for sunny spots.

ABOVE RIGHT: *Hydrangea aspera* is one of several hydrangea species with upright growth and very dramatic foliage.

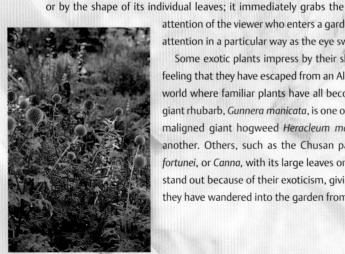

ABOVE LEFT: The hogweed, *Heracleum lehmannianum*, is a tall wide-spreading umbellifer. Its relationship to Queen Anne's lace is unmistakable.

ABOVE: *Eryngium giganteum*, known as Miss Willmott's ghost, is a biennial that self-sows itself easily, but rarely excessively, so it is welcome in the garden.

BELOW LEFT: The flowers, seed heads, and leaves of the thistle, *Echinops ritro*, are bold over a very long season.

OPPOSITE: The silver-leaved cardoon, *Cynara cardunculus*, and the ornamental rhubarb, *Rheum palmatum*, together create a dramatic spectacle among smaller-leaved plants.

BOLD AND EXOTIC PLANTS

"Bold" means to strike out, leap forward, to take risks, and engage in struggles that others do not. Understanding the word is a good way to think about the role of striking plants in the garden, and some of the problems that develop if they are not used appropriately.

Foliage in the garden has many aspects: overall plant form; leaf shape; leaf texture; leaf color; whether the leaf surface is glossy and thus light-reflecting or matte and thus light-absorbing; the way the leaves are arranged on the plant, and so on. A bold plant is one that leaps out from among the rest by virtue of its striking overall shape or by the shape of its individual leaves; it immediately grabs the attention of the viewer who enters a garden or focusses the attention in a particular way as the eye sweeps over a bed.

Some exotic plants impress by their sheer size, and the feeling that they have escaped from an Alice in Wonderland world where familiar plants have all become gigantic. The giant rhubarb, *Gunnera manicata*, is one of these; the much-maligned giant hogweed *Heracleum mantegazzianum*, is another. Others, such as the Chusan palm, *Trachycarpus fortunei*, or *Canna*, with its large leaves on an upright stem, stand out because of their exoticism, giving the impression they have wandered into the garden from another climate.

FAR LEFT: The large leaves of European seakale, *Crambe cordifolia*, and the umbrella plant, *Darmera peltata*, offer welcome variation among other more nondescript foliage.

LEFT: The shrubby *Mahonia* have striking hollylike leaves.

BELOW FAR LEFT: Given moist shade, an enormous number of fern species can be grown. This is *Dryopteris dilatata*.

BELOW LEFT: Spires of *Echium* dominate a vibrant planting that includes the silver cardoon, *Cynara cardunculus*.

BELOW: The Indian bean tree, *Catalpa bignonioides*, is large, but it can be kept pruned.

RIGHT: The tree fern (*Dicksonia antarctica*), skunk cabbage (*Lysichiton*), and the shuttlecock fern (*Matteuccia struthiopteris*) create an almost tropical ambience.

Other plants are considered exotic by virtue of having much larger leaves in relation to the overall size of the plant than we are accustomed to: the wide-spreading circular leaves of *Astilboides tabularis* for example, or the enormous leaves on *Hydrangea aspera* 'Macrophylla,' share this unusual, almost out-of-proportion quality. Other bold plants have sharp-edged, long, linear leaves that have a spiky dynamic, almost aggressive, quality that cannot fail to attract our attention, such as yuccas or cordylines.

Some plants are bold in more subtle ways. They may not seize our attention as soon as we walk into the garden, but they do hold it when we begin to peruse a bed. They draw attention because they have particularly fine or elegant foliage, qualities that can add a lift to their surroundings, especially useful in winter, early spring, or autumn, when there may be little else around to appreciate.

Thinking back to the definition of the word "bold," part of being bold is daring to take risks, which of course means that failure can be one result. Using bold and exotic plants in the garden can be risky: sometimes they seem to dominate their surroundings too much; or attract attention to the wrong part of the garden; or just not work well with surrounding plants. That is why we must consider carefully, and in some detail, how they can be used effectively in the garden.

EXOTICISM OR BOLDNESS ARE NOT
QUALITIES LIMITED TO ANY ONE
PARTICULAR GROUP OF PLANTS;
THEY ARE ALSO QUALITIES THAT,
TO SOME EXTENT, ARE IN THE EYE
OF THE BEHOLDER. IT COULD BE
SOMETHING ABOUT A SENSE OF
PRESENCE THAT THE WHOLE PLANT
HAS, THE SHAPE OF ITS FLOWER
HEADS, ITS LEAVES OR ITS
OVERALL FORM. IN THE END YOU
MUST MAKE UP YOUR OWN MIND.

QUALITIES

OPPOSITE: *Fascicularia pitcairnifolia* is a hardy member of the pineapple family, or bromeliads.

ABOVE: *Magnolia grandiflora* is one of the finest of the evergreen bold plants.

FOCAL POINTS

Some of the most useful bold and exotic plants are those that make good focal points, plants that immediately catch and hold the attention. While a great many bold plants may do this, I want to concentrate here on those that have the relatively unusual quality of being symmetrical, at least when young—these are the most highly rated of bold plants. Their ability to attract attention and their symmetry make them absolutely invaluable in gardens where there is an element of formality, as they can be used as "punctuation marks," as a period at the end of a long vista, for example, or as commas, or parentheses marking out regular and distinct intervals along a path or wall or other feature, such as a long flower bed.

The most popular such plant, certainly of recent years, has been the exotic *Cordyline australis* (New Zealand cabbage tree), with its rosette of radiating straplike leaves. While it is resistant to strong winds in mild maritime areas, it is not especially hardy to cold winds or frosts, which limits its usefulness. Species of yucca, such as *Yucca gloriosa*, are hardier and stay symmetrical for several years, until they grow side shoots.

Growing a focal point plant in an ornamental urn or a pot is a very common way of treating these plants, using the container either as a formal centerpiece to an area or at the end of some kind of formal path. While growing a plant in a container does make it more vulnerable to frosts (*see* Containers *page* 102), the root restriction does make it easier to keep the plants small and juvenile in growth form and thus maintain their symmetry for longer. Such containerized plants are relatively easy to carry indoors or into a frostfree greenhouse for the winter to protect them from the cold.

If you have the means to bring a focal-point plant inside over the winter, the range of possibilities can be greatly extended—to agaves, for example, the classic focal

point plants of so many countries that enjoy a balmy climate. Their dangerously spiny rosettes place them among the most beautifully symmetrical of all plants. The aloes are less symmetrical, softer looking, tender succulents that also make good urn plants. The use of succulents like aloes and agaves in containers is an especially good idea if there is any likelihood watering may be erratic.

Where there is shade, and regular watering can be maintained, a hosta makes a good urn plant, as an alternative to the sun-loving plants mentioned so far, especially the majestic *Hosta sieboldiana*. The Chusan palm (*Trachycarpus fortunei*) can be used as a focal point in areas where the climate is mild, and where a plant with a strong vertical element is considered necessary. While it is slow growing, a young Chusan palm that has not yet formed a trunk is still very useful as a large focal point, and it grows well in containers.

PLANTS WITH PRESENCE

In a sense, all bold and exotic plants are plants with presence. Here, however, I would like to consider those that attract attention within the garden, but which are not symmetrical enough to fit comfortably into the kind of formal settings described on the previous pages .

Large spaces can be rendered magnificent by the addition of a *Araucaria araucana* (the monkey-puzzle tree), which even when still quite small has immense character. *Cortaderia selloana* (pampas grass), looks majestic if given enough space, which it must be said it usually is not. It needs space around it to be appreciated and seen at its best, and several planted closely together in clumps generally look better than single isolated specimens.

Smaller spaces—the kind of garden size that most of us have to work with—can be transformed with a distinctively shaped shrub or, on a more seasonal basis, by one of the grander perennials or grasses, plants that combine size with striking foliage. While there are only a few hardy shrubs with really distinctive form, or that combine neat shape with quality foliage, there are plenty of perennials that do; indeed, most large perennials have very elegant foliage. The problem with the latter, of course, is that they die back in the winter, leaving the borders empty and bare.

Among the choice of shrubs, one of the best is *Fatsia japonica* (Japanese aralia), with its big evergreen hand-shaped leaves, or the more upright *Aralia elata* (Japanese angelica tree), which has huge deciduous leaves divided into two sets of leaflets. Both are so distinctive that nothing else is needed to add elegance to a small area such as a courtyard. Among perennials, *Heracleum*

mantegazzianum (giant hogweed) has immense presence, but is unpopular for the rash it causes some people in hot weather. Not quite so tall, but still magnificent, are some other related plants such as angelica, the impressive silvery-leaved *Cynara cardunculus* (cardoon), or the biennial *Onopordium acanthium* (Scotch thistle). *Macleaya cordata* (plume poppy) is one of the best of the taller perennials for adding dignity to planting. Its leaves are a shape quite unlike anything else, vaguely like a fig, and a subtle green-gray color.

There are also plenty of other perennials with presence that are lower growing, all of them, whether they are chosen for their flowers or leaf color, useful for combining with other species. Their long season and strong form help to anchor less distinctive plants, and they provide a sense |of structure in a scheme. *Rheum*, or rhubarbs, for example, dominate by virtue of large, wide-spreading and usually distinctively colored leaves, while the silvery leaves of *Melianthus major* (honey bush) impose through a sense of sheer quality.

BIG LEAVES

Some plants appear exotic through having foliage of unusual size, unusual at least for hardy plants in temperate climates. Such are the *Rheum* species, or the ornamental rhubarbs, just discussed, and the even more impressive *Gunnera*, of which *G. manicata* (giant rhubarb) has by far the largest leaves of any hardy plant. These are basically waterside or bog plants, as are most other genera of perennials with exceptionally large leaves: *Darmera* (umbrella plant), *Rodgersia* and *Astilboides*. This tends to limit their use in the garden to moist environments. But they can make a splendid accompaniment to water, and their horizontally held leaves can be effectively contrasted with the upright linear leaves of waterside irises, reedy grasses, or reedmace (the *Typha* species).

With some imagination and technical ingenuity, it is possible to use these large-leaved perennials in novel ways. I have occasionally seen them growing in channels running down steep slopes, where it is possible to look up through the leaves, seeing them backlit—a completely different experience from how they are normally seen.

OPPOSITE: *Darmera peltata* (umbrella plant) will grow in moderately moist conditions, but does best in waterside mud.

ABOVE LEFT: *Paulownia tomentosa* (the empress tree), can be kept small by frequent cutting, making a first-rate foliage plant.

ABOVE CENTER: The plume poppies (*Macleaya*) are some of the finest perennial foliage plants and gratifyingly easy to grow.

ABOVE RIGHT: *Actinidia deliciosa* (the Chinese gooseberry) is a large climber with tropically large leaves.

RIGHT: For those with sheltered gardens and moist acid soils, there are a host of large-leaved **rhododendrons** to choose from.

Large-leaved shrubs offer more variety in shape, such as Japanese aralia (*Fatsia japonica)*, or the common fig (*Ficus carica*), which also has hand-shaped leaves but a bigger, bulkier habit, and is deciduous. More upright in habit are the various hydrangeas, varieties of the variable *H. aspera*, whose wide, very hairy leaves hang from erect stems, forming an excellent foil for the white and mauve flower heads in mid summer. Woody plants with larger leaves than these tend to be less hardy, and so need careful positioning in the garden. There are a good number of rhododendron species with magnificent leaves, glossy dark green with wonderfully brown "fur," known as indumentum, on the undersides or coating the young growth, but they need acid soils that never dry out and protection from cold or strong winds. *Rhododendron sinogrande* has the largest leaves, up to 15 inches.

Of other large-leaved woody-stemmed plants, *Paulownia tomentosa* (empress tree) is perhaps the most versatile; not only are the leaves very big, it is possible to treat it as herbaceous in climates too cold for regular survival of the top growth. If it is cut back, its leaves are substantially bigger than if it is grown as a tree, up to 20 inches across.

Large-leaved climbers are some of the most exciting bold plants. Species such as *Actinidia deliciosa* (Chinese gooseberry), *Aristolochia macrophylla* (Dutchman's pipe), or the relative of the Japanese vine, *Vitis coignetiae,* form spectacularly large plants with time, and even when their overall growth is restricted, their big leaves bring a touch of tropical exuberance to wherever they are positioned.

TOP: Spiky foliage plants such as **cordyline** and **phormium** always create impact, but often only thrive in milder climates. Euphorbia and **primula** provide tropical-looking underplanting.

ABOVE: *Agave americana* 'Variegata' is not hardy but this magnificent plant can be enjoyed in the garden if it is grown in a container and brought indoors in winter.

ABOVE CENTER RIGHT: The long-stemmed *Yucca rostrata* is one of many of this impressive group of plants that are surprisingly cold-hardy and are thus easy to maintain.

ABOVE BOTTOM RIGHT: *Chamaerops humilis* (the dwarf fan palm) is a shrubby palm that is hardy in milder temperate climates.

BELOW RIGHT: *Eryngium bourgatii* is a good spiky plant for a dry front-of-border situation, or to combine with grasses and drought-tolerant plants for a steppe or Mediterranean feel.

BOTTOM RIGHT: By mid to late summer the branched stems of *Eryngium bourgatii* are crowned with blue conelike flowers surrounded by stars of jagged spikes of stunning metallic hue.

SPIKES AND ROSETTES

We have already seen how certain plants with a very symmetrical habit can be used as focal point plants. Most of these species have linear leaves arranged around a single central growth point. As time goes on, however, most develop other growth points and become less symmetrical, although they retain a great deal of character. These, and others with spiky leaves, can be very useful, largely because they are such a dramatic contrast to most other garden plants. They also have a dynamic quality, a sense of restless movement. Some can almost be aggressive.

A similar dynamic effect can be created with the dwarf fan palm *Chamaerops humilis*, which forms multiple stems clothed with palmate leaves that thrust spiky tips in all directions. This and the yuccas do very well in hot, dry situations, making them ideal for conveying a Mediterranean or semidesert climate, growing among scattered rocks on a slope, for example, with the addition of terracotta containers spilling scarlet pelargonium completing the illusion.

While they do not need or particularly like hot, dry sites, some other plants can be combined with yucca to give the impression of a sun-baked hillside. Examples are red hot pokers, or *Kniphofia* hybrids, and Jacob's rod (*Asphodeline lutea*), both of which have rosettes of linear leaves and upward-thrusting spires of flowers, and species of sea holly, or eryngium, which have spiny-looking leaves and exotic-looking flowers. *Eryngium agavifolium* is most commonly available, and its rosettes of spiny-edged leaves and thimble-shaped flower heads make it an instant focus of attention wherever it is planted.

A combination of these spiky-looking plants can be used to create a strong sense of illusion. However, they can look very restless together, so the impression of semidesert needs to be thorough for the mix to be successful. Alternatively, they can be combined with softer-looking plants to calm them down and dilute their energy.

Of the rosette plants, one which has become increasingly popular over recent years is *Phormium tenax*, the New Zealand flax, with wide, strap-shaped leaves arching out from a growth point at ground level. Its popularity is also due to the wide range of varieties available, with leaves in many different colors and patterns of variegation. It can make a very decorative contrast with other plants in the garden, but it does need space, becoming very substantial with time, something which many who plant it appear to fail to realize.

Finally, it is worth considering plants like iris or crocosmia, which have linear leaves which thrust upward. They introduce a note of dynamism to perennial plantings as they are so dramatically different in shape from other perennials.

FINE LINES

Most garden plants have relatively undistinguished shapes: the majority of shrubs have amorphous outlines, and many perennials, while often developing various characteristic shapes in the course of the annual cycle of growth, have leaves that create a very similar impression from afar. However colorful the planting plan is, if no plants of characteristic form are included, the overall effect can be rather uninspiring and dull.

The easiest way to liven up such a planting is with the inclusion of plants with linear foliage, which will break up the overall mass of amorphous shapes and elliptical leaf shapes. Plants like irises, hemerocallis, grasses, and sedges are all very useful for this, quite apart from the value of their flowers, and they can be used as graphic accents to punctuate and break up large stretches of planting. Some linear-leaved plants are particularly desirable for the elegance of their lines; for example, the evergreen weeping sedge *Carex pendula,* with its rosette of arching dark leaves and wiry flower stems bending gently under the weight of the catkinlike flower heads is invaluable.

On a somewhat larger scale, some plants can be used to introduce a bolder sense of line—bamboos are impressive, their stems usually starting off straight and bending slightly under the weight of leaves farther up. Older specimens, which develop a thick mass of stems at the base of the plant, create a particularly bold outline, an effect that continues into the winter. Those with coloured stems are especially effective, such as the black *Phyllostachys nigra* or yellow *P. aureosulcata.*

Most striking of all are those plants that have a distinct vertical quality, which makes them not only stand out, but also provides a bold variation on the pattern of growth of most plants. The Italian cypress, *Cupressus sempervirens*, is one of the best known, but the smaller juniper *Juniperus scopulorum* 'Skyrocket' is more suitable for cold climates.

Many perennials have flower spikes that have a spirelike dimension; when grown in groups, they make an eye-catching addition to the garden. Foxtail lilies (*Eremurus*), with their 6-foot spires, are exceptional and not always easy, but foxgloves, especially *Digitalis ferruginea*, are effective and much more versatile, as are the yellow and red hot pokers (*Kniphofia*) and clustered pale blue or white spires of *Veronicastrum virginicum*.

LEFT: These drumstick flower heads are of an *Allium* species —the ornamental garlics. Their narrow tapering stems provide light relief among perennials of much denser form.

RIGHT: *Phyllostachys nigra*, the very popular black-stemmed bamboo, is an excellent plant for providing strong vertical accents in confined spaces.

FAR RIGHT: Fine leaves of grasses contrast with the large-leaved clary sage (*Salvia sclarea var. turkestanica*) and the spires of foxtail lilies (*Eremurus*).

BELOW: A successful border is not just packed with colorful flowers, but has plenty of other interest to sustain it over a long season. Here the gray-green swords of **iris** leaves and the flowerless seed-head-topped *Allium* stalks provide good vertical features and a structure that will remain in place for most of the year, long after the flowers have faded.

For the end of summer in cool spots, there is bugbane (*Cimicifuga*) in white or pink. Such perennials not only need to be grown in loose groups to be most effective, but should ideally be scattered through the garden as well—the resulting sense of rhythm creates a powerful sense of visual unity.

Some grasses have good upright flower and seed spikes, too, and of all non-woody plants the feather reed grass *Calamagrostis* x *acutiflora* 'Karl Foerster' is probably the best vertical element, looking good for at least nine months of the year.

ELEGANCE

Certain plants have qualities that make them really stand out from the rest, but which are strangely difficult to categorize. Their shape may be a bit unusual or their leaves have a distinct quality; quite often the combination of fine shape and leaves come together to create a feeling that the whole is greater than the sum of the parts. "Elegance" or "grace" are often the words used to describe this, and it is the sheer good design of such plants that makes them bold.

The shrubs known as mahonias are a good example. Their holly-like leaves (actually leaflets), radiating out from an upright main stem, are arranged in such a way that their shape is emphasized. *Griselina littoralis* is another, with distinct light green and very shiny leaves held at an angle to the stem, which seems almost deliberately designed to show them off at their best.

Among the perennials, the silvery-toothed leaves of *Melianthus major* (honey bush) are well displayed in a dignified clump (on young plants at any rate) that generates equal feelings of admiration as the shrubs already suggested. The smaller leaves of *Sanguisorba* (burnet) have a similar quality, and are especially attractive when they form part of a neat clump in the early part of the growing season. Very different in shape are the pinnate leaves of peonies, which are effectively displayed by the moundlike shapes of the plants.

The effect of a mound of graceful leaves is perhaps most clearly illustrated by *Euphorbia mellifera* (honey spurge), a shrubby species that does not look very distinguished when young, but which when older makes a fine sight, every leaf seemingly in just the right place. A similar effect is created by *Helleborus foetidus*, with its evergreen mound of narrowly palmate leaves. Plants like this should be grown in situations where they will not be cramped and thus lose much of their shape and character.

More upright are *Veratrum*, which have pleated leaves (very unusual among non-tropical plants) on erect stems, which makes them stand out over a long season. Some ferns combine good leaf shape with good overall shape, generally forming a vase, but *Osmunda regalis* (the royal fern) is more vertical. A majestic sight by water, its elegance is made bolder by the uniqueness of its combination of characteristics. Finally, bamboos should not be forgotten in this category. All are undeniably graceful plants as they mature and, being evergreen, are worthy of a key position in the garden.

LEFT: The bamboo *Phyllostachys aureosulcata* is one of those plants that needs to be positioned so its unique features can be examined at close range.

ABOVE TOP: A mahonia combines bulk with elegant and unusual leaves. It makes a good courtyard plant.

ABOVE BOTTOM: *Euphorbia mellifera* (honey spurge) has neat leaves with a fine midrib. The plant forms a rounded shape eventually.

OPPOSITE: Waterside planting is the best way to show off the majestic royal fern, *Osmunda regalis*, which, given time and space, will form large clumps.

FAR LEFT: `Viburnum rhytidophyllum` (the
leatherleaf viburnum), underplanted with `Scilla
sibirica`, becomes the focus of interest in
a spring garden.

BELOW FAR LEFT: `Araucaria araucana`, the monkey
puzzle tree, is fascinating whether viewed
closely or from afar.

LEFT: The glossy leaves of `Magnolia grandiflora`
are quite different in tone from those of most
evergreens, with a yellow-russet tone.
Consequently they have a warmer appearance.

BOTTOM LEFT: The stone pine, `Pinus pinea`, is
a classic Mediterranean tree with a distinctive
umbrella shape. Hardy much further north, it
ought to be more widely grown.

BELOW RIGHT: Birches, species of `Betula`, are
invaluable for all-season interest, and for
a tree, take up little space.

EVERGREENS

Evergreens are somehow the quintessential bold plants. Some might even try to argue that a bold-leaved plant that retreats underground every autumn (as perennials do) or drops its leaves (as deciduous plants do) is somehow only a bold plant part time. An evergreen has the advantage of not only reminding us of life in the depths of winter but of providing a sense of continuity in the garden.

The problem with evergreens, though, is twofold: one is that because they are always there looking more or less the same, we get bored with them; and the other is that certain evergreens have always been so popular that they have become clichés. Think of the cypresses that bring a dreary suburban look to so many areas, or the laurel hedges that were once popular and are now often massively overgrown.

Exotic plants always have an advantage in that they carry with them a sense of novelty and surprise. One only has to hope that they will not become too popular and thus lose some of their impact. The monkey puzzle tree (*Araucaria araucana*) has been around a long time, but it is still uncommon enough, and dramatic enough, to create a sense of surprise when it is seen. Less strange, but still definite crowd pleasers, are a number of other conifers with outstanding foliage that will probably never become commonplace—the Himalayan white pine *Pinus wallichiana* with its long needles, for example, and Mexican species such as *P. patula* and *P. montezumae*, which have longer needles still, or species of *Podocarpus*, which have extravagantly thick and somewhat widely spaced needles. Such plants look bold from afar and reward closer attention.

During the winter, any green is going to stand out from its all-too-often dreary surroundings, so something that is quite inconspicuous during the summer might well be worth the space during the winter, such as the otherwise thoroughly dull iris *I. foetidissima*. It is much more rewarding, however, to choose plants on the basis of real quality and to position them to make the most of what they have to offer. Mahonias, for example, have interesting foliage and can be planted in situations, such as near a path or doorway, where their form and the scent of their flowers will be appreciated.

While the green of most evergreens tends to be consistent, and usually dark, it helps to be aware of the subtleties between various plants that makes all the difference between something run of the mill and something outstanding, such as the golden tones and glossiness of *Magnolia grandiflora*, or the rough texture and neat shape of the foliage of the leatherleaf viburnum, *V. rhytidophyllum*.

TREES AND SHRUBS

Trees and shrubs, being large, create a major impact in the garden, and sometimes beyond, too. Having a tree or larger shrub that makes a real statement sets the tone for the whole garden. It also tends to dominate the space around it, so that really bold woody plants are often grown as specimens, in splendid isolation. Arguably, this may be the best way to appreciate their special qualities.

Some trees stand out because of their exceptional shape. The dogwood *Cornus controversa*, with its unusual wedding-cake shape, is one, while the hornbeam *Carpinus betulus* 'Fastigiata' has a pattern of upright sweeping branches that is exceptionally beautiful. Many conifers also develop a distinctive shape, although often only after some years of growth. Those with a 'Christmas tree' shape, though, mainly species of fir (*Abies*) and spruce (*Picea*), develop their characteristics relatively quickly. The elegantly narrow *P.omorika* fits into a small garden and creates quite an impact with its shape, as does the spectacular weeping *P. breweriana*, with its pendent branches. Other trees appear bold or exotic because of the size or style of their leaves. Species of the Indian bean tree (*Catalpa*) and the empress tree (*Paulownia*) are useful for this quality, and have attractive flowers as an added extra. The largest leaves of any hardy tree are those of the poplar (*Populus lasiocarpa*), which can grow up to a foot long, and being a poplar it establishes fast.

Few shrubs develop strong or elegant shapes. Of those that do, most have upward-growing stems and an attractively arching habit, such as the Himalyan honeysuckle (*Leycesteria formosa*) or *Neillia thibetica*. Some combine an upright habit with large leaves, such as the doubly pinnate aralia, which eventually sucker to form stands of slightly menacing stems, armed with vicious spines. *Viburnum plicatum* 'Mariesii' , the Japanese snowball, is one of the few to develop an interesting horizontal shape, with a layered branching pattern . Bamboos are shrubs in garden design terms, as they take up the same space and they usually have good form. *Chusquea culeou* is possibly the finest for overall shape, forming a dense clump with canes that arch as it grows.

Most bold shrubs are bold because of their leaf shape, size, or texture. Hydrangeas nearly always have good foliage, as do rhododendrons. The glossiness of camellia leaves, and the relatively neat shape of many varieties, deserves recognition, too, as do hollies, which, if grown unencumbered by neighbors, develop a fine pyramidal shape. Shrubs that are bold through having large leaves tend to be very sensitive to wind, which limits where they can be used. *Fatsia japonica* (Japanese aralia) is one of the hardiest such shrubs, but only to frost, not winds. In exposed situations,shape is a more appropriate characteristic to focus on.

TOP: *Aesculus*, or buckeyes, are fine foliage and flowering shrubs for gardens with space to accommodate their suckering habit.

ABOVE: *Hydrangea quercifolia* has exceptionally fine leaves that turn red in autumn. It is usefully tolerant of light shade.

RIGHT: The potentially large-growing *Catalpa bignonioides* (Indian bean tree) can be kept small by pruning.

OPPOSITE: A fully grown *Catalpa* is a magnificent sight; its sculptural branching habit looks good at all times of year.

PERENNIALS

It is perennials that provide the majority of bold and exotic plants for gardens in temperate climates. Perennials die back in the winter to ground level, only exposing their leaves and stems to the outside world when warm enough. It is therefore possible to grow really dramatic plants in places that are too cold for trees or shrubs.

The advantage of perennials is that each species develops a clear and distinct shape, so the experienced gardener can identify a plant from its outline alone. Trees are like this as well, whereas shrubs tend not to be; being more amorphous in growth, their overall shape is often dictated by how they can fit into their immediate surroundings. As a general rule, the shape of a perennial is linked to its flowering season and its habitat, irrespective of neighbors and position.

Early-flowering perennials tend to be from shaded habitats, and be low growing, even ground hugging, although there are some very good bold species: the hellebores, for example, especially the taller ones, like *H. argutifolius* and *H.foetidus*; or those that are regarded as bold through having glossy leaves, like the wandflower *Galax urceolata*.

Perennials that flower in early to midsummer tend to form low rounded clumps, such as the cranesbills or hardy geraniums, few being striking for form alone. It is among the later-flowering

TOP: Moist soil gives opportunity to grow a range of large-leaved plants, *Gunnera manicata*, *Hosta sieboldiana*, and *Kirengeshoma palmata* among them.

ABOVE LEFT: *Veratrum viridis* grows alongside a *Macleaya* (plume poppy) and a hosta.

RIGHT: Some perennials have distinctive flower shapes that are a feature in their own right. This is the thistle *Echinops ritro* in midsummer.

FAR RIGHT: The spires of *Eremurus*, or foxtail lilies, are highly effective vertical elements of a planting, over a long season. They do best on very well-drained soils.

perennials that the most dramatic shapes are to be found. Late summer- and autumn-flowering perennials have a strong tendency to be taller, which often results in their having two distinct shapes in the course of a single growing season: the earlier short clump of leaves and the later taller stems, topped with flowers, that often have a highly characteristic form. A good example are the globe thistles, *Echinops*, which have a large clump of striking, jagged-edged leaves through late spring and early summer, sending up straight stems to flower in midsummer. These are immediately noticeable for their globe-shaped flower heads, which stand out among less well-defined shapes. Other examples are the big *Eupatorium* like *E. purpureum* subsp. *maculatum*, which emerge from relatively inconspicuous mounds to form robust, tall clumps, with flattish umbels of pink flowers. Even after they have finished flowering, the majority of these upright growers continue to look good well into the winter.

The other main category of bold and exotic perennials are those that produce very large leaves from ground level. These are almost entirely plants of moist or waterside

habitats, where they can afford to grow expansive and lush. *Gunnera*, *Rheum* (including the culinary rhubarb), and *Rodgersia* are among the most dramatic. From less moist, shaded habitats come hostas, some of which have big enough leaves to fall into the category of bold plants, especially cultivars or hybrids of *H. sieboldiana*.

LEFT: *Cortaderia selloana* 'Rendatleri' is one of the magnificent pampas grasses, which need plenty of space to be effective.

GRASSES

Grasses have the huge advantage that they nearly all look interesting over a long season, with many adding a fine structural element to the garden for a good nine months of the year, their appearance often subtly changing as they age. The vast majority are also remarkably tolerant of a wide range of conditions, full sunlight being the only vital requirement for most. Some have good-quality evergreen foliage, with many of the species also offering attractively variegated cultivars, but it is the flower heads, maturing to the long-lasting seed heads, that are their main feature. Given the prevalence of grasses in natural environments, the addition of grasses to the garden planting scheme tends to evoke different natural habitats, in particular those places where grasses are an important, if not vital, part of the visual appeal: meadows, the prairie, the coast, marshland.

The archetypal bold grass is pampas grass, *Cortaderia selloana*, with its large clump of dark evergreen leaves and in winter the long plumelike seed heads. It has, however, become so widely used as to become a cliché, which is a shame since it is a magnificent plant. Personally, I feel it is most effectively used as just one element among many in a border, occupying the sort of shape and position that a shrub would have in a mixed bed, toward the back and surrounded by smaller and gently contrasting plants. It can also look magnificent in a planting alongside shrubs of a similar or larger size, in autumn especially, when the silver of the plumes is seen alongside fiery autumn foliage and colorful berries. It is, however, all too often unsuitably grown as a specimen, on its own in splendid isolation in the middle of a small lawn, in cramped surroundings that simply do not do it justice. Several plants in a loose clump in a very large expanse of lawn in an open setting can be quite magnificent, though.

We should learn from the descent of this magnificent plant into clichédom, if only to make sure other equally good species do not go the same way, such as *Miscanthus sinensis*, which is rapidly becoming the most popular ornamental grass. Smaller than pampas grass, and more graceful, *Miscanthus* is available in a bewildering number of varieties, which vary considerably in size from about 20 inches tall to over 6 feet, and with flower/seed heads that vary in color from silvery white to pinkish brown. *Miscanthus* is not only a plant that makes a real impact, but it is extraordinarily elegant, too, from late summer to late winter, especially when its plumes are all bent sideways at exactly the same angle in the wind. Smaller grasses can make bold statements in more confined spaces, especially those with clumps of tufted foliage, such as the weeping sedge *Carex pendula* or the elegant variegated Japanese sedge *C. morrowii* 'Variegata.'

RIGHT: 'Yakushima Dwarf' is a small-growing form of the late-flowering *Miscanthus sinensis*. The tree is *Cedrus libani* subsps. *atlantica* 'Glauca'.

OPPOSITE: *Stipa gigantea* (giant feather grass) may be imposing, but it has a transparent quality that allows other plants to be seen through it.

ANNUALS AND TENDER PLANTS

Victorian gardeners were very fond of using bold and exotic plants in temporary summer bedding plans, a practice that is enjoying something of a revival. Summer bedding usually consists of low-growing plants that are either annual (that is, they only live naturally for one year) or which grow so fast they are treated as annuals and discarded at the end of the year. Since most are grown for their color and are of uniform height, the Victorians used larger, more architectural plants alongside them. Most of these would be primarily foliage plants, although a few, notably *Abutilon* (flowering maple) and *Brugmansia* (angel's trumpet), the shrubby species of *Datura*, had both bold foliage and exotic-looking flowers. These architectural specimens were tender shrubs or perennials that were carefully dug up and moved inside to protect them through the winter. Bold tender plants, those which can be grown outside during the warmer summer months only, and exotic tropical plants, that grow so fast they can become a feature in the garden only a few months after germination, have enormous potential to spice up plantings of traditional flowering annuals and bedding. Some of the true annuals are also potential bold plants.

To consider the true annuals first, the best known and loved must be the sunflower (*Helianthus annuus*) but the varieties commonly grown are so incredibly tall they can look out of place in most planting plans. There are, however, seed strains available now that grow to a much better-proportioned 3 to 6 feet, and whose large flowers and big triangular leaves make a powerful statement when surrounded by smaller and more intricate plants. Similar in their exotic effect, and in their combination of strong flower head shape and overall form, are the innumerable varieties of *Amaranthus* (which incidentally is one of the most widely grown and nutritious tropical vegetables). They have an upright habit of growth and either upright or very pendent flower heads packed with tiny pink, red, yellow, or orange flowers.

There are also several grasses that are grown for their combination of foliage and flower/seed heads—ornamental varieties of maize (*Zea mays*), for example. The very wide strap-shaped leaves make a wonderfully exotic statement when they are grown among other large-leaved or exuberantly colorful annuals, while the rather smaller-growing *Panicum miliacium* 'Violaceum' is an ornamental millet whose attractive seed heads can be left as a winter food resource for wild birds.

The perennial cannas, too, combine erect growth with bold leaves and very brightly colored flowers, qualities that have guaranteed their place among some of the most profusely planted species in warm climates. The wide, roughly oval-shaped leaves are usually a fresh shade of green, but there are also variegated and purple forms available. *C. iridiflora* is a particularly dramatic variety, with bright pink flowers on a plant that is exceptionally lush, both in form and in the green of its leaves.

Boldest of all tender and annual plants are those are grown purely for their foliage effect. Ensete ventricosum (syn. Musa ensete) is an ornamental banana that grows so fast from seed it can be grown as an annual, or alternately chopped down every autumn and treated as herbaceous. Musa basjoo is a true banana whose roots are frost hardy and, in climates where winter temperatures only rarely fall below freezing, can be successfully grown outside if the trunk is wrapped in insulating material (see Choosing and Siting Bold Plants pages 98–101). There is nothing like the foliage of bananas to make you feel you are in the tropics.

Many of the palm species that are grown as conservatory plants can be grown outside for the summer, which was a particularly favorite Victorian practice—for example, species of date palm, or *Phoenix*, seem to thrive on an annual vacation outside. The foliage is of the pinnate kind (a long central midrib with leaflets on each side) a leaf shape no truly hardy palm has, species of *Trachycarpus*, *Chamaedorea* and other hardy palms all having palmate, or hand-shaped, leaves with divisions arising from a central point.

Several exceptionally good foliage plants are on the borderline of being hardy. In mild areas they can be treated as normal garden plants; in slightly colder places they need some winter insulation. But in more severe climates they would need to be treated as subtropical plants, and every winter dug up and moved into a greenhouse or conservatory for protection. *Melianthus major* (the honey bush) has silver toothed pinnate foliage of exceptional quality that contrasts beautifully with the dark greens so common among warm climate plants. Slightly less hardy is the rice-paper plant, *Tetrapanax papyrifera*, with huge, furry, gray-green palmate leaves. An annual, and even bigger, alternative to the latter is the castor oil plant, *Ricinus communis*, with large palmate leaves; it is most frequently seen as the centerpiece to a bedding plan.

If you have a sheltered garden, it is worth considering which other conservatory or house plants can be stood outside, a practice that does much to help keep them free of pests like red spider and whitefly and which promotes even, firm growth. Most plants from subtropical regions can be treated in this way: *Schefflera* (otherwise known as *Aralia*), *Dracaena*, species of fig, and cordylines all add foliage shapes, and sometimes colors, to the garden that are impossible to find among hardy plants. Any species with what appear to be physically tough, leathery leaves is probably suitable. Those lower-growing plants with thinner, more easily torn, leaves are quite possibly tropicals, which might be more risky outside in a cool temperate summer.

LEFT: *Phoenix*, or date, palms make superb centerpieces. Though not fully hardy, they can be brought inside during long hard winters, or protected *in situ* by materials such as burlap during shorter cold snaps.

ABOVE: Exotic foliage is set off well by gravel and other hard landscaping. Not only do these surfaces look attractive, they are also invaluable for reflecting the heat exotic plants love.

OPPOSITE: The unmistakable foliage of the banana, *Musa bajoo*, dominates a planting including mauve-purple *Verbena bonariensis*.

THE FEATURES AND QUALITIES OF THESE FINE AND VARIED PLANTS ARE MANY AND INSPIRING. EVERY GARDEN AND GARDENER CAN BRING SOME DIFFERENT ASPECT INTO PLAY: THE GRACE OF DELICATE, FEATHERY SPECIES, THE STATUESQUE PRESENCE OF THE LARGEST AND BOLDEST, AND CROWNING EVERY QUALITY, THE RUSTLE AND SWAY OF THE STEMS AND FOLIAGE MOVING *EN MASSE*.

IN YOUR GARDEN

OPPOSITE: A large clump of *Miscanthus sinensis* is still at its best while everything around it is beginning to take on the shades of autumn.

ABOVE: Dark-leaved **cannas** add an exotic touch while clipped **hollies** make a year-round statement.

SPECIMEN PLANTS

A specimen plant is one that is grown alone, in splendid isolation, usually in the middle of an area of lawn, although paving, decking, or gravel might be more contemporary possibilities. Specimen planting is a good way of showing off something really special, something with exceptionally striking form and good foliage. If something is to be used as a specimen plant, it goes without saying that it must look good, from all angles and at all seasons.

Certain trees are classics for that middle-of-the-lawn situation; *Araucaria araucana* (the monkey puzzle tree) is one of the boldest at any age. Many other majestic conifers are also suitable, along with broad-leaved trees with striking foliage and shape, such as *Paulownia tomentosa* (the empress tree) or *Magnolia grandiflora*. Such trees are only suitable for a large space of course. Small trees lack that quality of grandeur that is so vital in a good specimen plant, so for restricted spaces it is better to look at those few shrubs that have good growth pattern. *Cornus controversa* (giant dogwood), with its wedding-cake tiered branches, is an exceptional one with a treelike habit, while *Viburnum plicatum* 'Mariesii' (doublefile viburnum) is more untidily layered and has a more spreading shape.

Something more upright often looks better in medium-sized spaces, such as *Aralia elata* (Japanese angelica tree), whose suckering clump of spiny stems bear clusters of much-divided leaves. This is a plant that stands out not just for being magnificent, but also for having an almost bizarre appearance. Mahonias have pinnate foliage, too, but unlike aralias (which turn to dead sticks in the winter) they are evergreen. Their upward-swept growth and fine foliage make them ideal specimens for the smaller garden and, given that they tolerate some shade, for more confined spaces, too, such as courtyards. They can look bare around the base, so consider lower planting around the bottom of the plants. Often grown in smaller spaces is *Fatsia japonica* (Japanese aralia), which has a very different growth pattern, being very rounded, with large leathery leaves. It will grow well in a corner or against a wall, but can also be relied upon to form a nicely shaped specimen grown in isolation. Similar in this respect is the dwarf palm *Chamaerops humilis*, with its multiple stems of hand-shaped leaves.

Perennials, which disappear underground in winter, may not be the obvious choice as specimen plants, but they can be summer-only specimens. *Macleaya microcarpa* has the required qualities of size and and majesty, and if grown surrounded, and thus restricted, by pavement or mown grass, its running habit will not be a nuisance. *Heracleum mantegazzianum* (giant hogweed) is a superb specimen, too, as its enormous dead remains will stand for the winter.

Some of the bamboos make good specimens, but only if they can be trusted not to run: *Chusquea culeou* is the best, forming a very tight and elegant clump. Pampas grass is often grown as a specimen, often unsuccessfully, but other grasses tend not to lend themselves to this.

OPPOSITE: *Aralia elata*, known as the devil's walking stick for the vicious spines on the stem, is dramatic at any stage of growth.

ABOVE: *Magnolia grandiflora* is often grown as a wall shrub, but it is hardier than many imagine and deserves to be grown as a tree.

RIGHT: *Cortaderia selloana* 'Rendatleri' (pampas grass), is a quintessential specimen plant, but only if there is a large area of lawn around it.

COMBINING BOLD AND EXOTIC PLANTS WITH OTHER PLANTS

Bold and exotic plants will in most cases be grown alongside others. In doing so, we must be clear what we hope to achieve. These plants attract attention—that is their primary purpose after all—and their fine form and foliage must carry a planting plan through a longer season than flowering plants will, and they should contribute a sense of structure and rhythm to a planting. What they must not do, however, is attract so much attention they draw it away completely from everything else around them.

Plants that are really striking can be used to seize the eye of the beholder, and thus make them look in the direction you want them to look in. Having been attracted

by one element in a group of plants, the viewer will then hopefully be encouraged to look around at what else there is. Good, strong verticals, such as bamboos, or perennials with upward-thrusting spikes like mulleins (*Verbascum*), are good at doing just this. Exotic foliage grabs the attention, too—one palm among more typically temperate-zone shrubs will instantly leap out. Plants that seem to yell "look here" are useful as specific focal points, like the classic use of a cordyline or an agave in an urn positioned at the end of a pathway. Dramatic-looking plants glimpsed through openings in boundaries such as gates or gaps in hedges will make the viewer want

to walk on farther and see what else is in that part of the garden. However, there is a danger that a striking plant will focus so much attention it leads the viewer to ignore everything else. Just as bright pink flowers at the far end of a garden leap immediately into sight, foreshortening the perspective, so are bold and exotic plants best placed so that they beckon you on, rather than being revealed all at once.

TOP: Bold-leaved perennials make the most of a damp patch: *Persicaria* (bottle brush), *Thalictrum* (meadow rue), *Angelica*, *Verbascum* (mullein), and the bamboo *Phyllostachys bambusoides*.

ABOVE LEFT: *Darmera peltata* (umbrella plant) will always attract attention.

LEFT: On a dry site, grasses, spiky *Verbascum* (mullein), and the distinctive whorled flowers of a *Phlomis* (Jerusalem sage) provide interest in a planting of uniform height.

TOP RIGHT: The pleated leaves of *Veratrum album* act as punctuation.

ABOVE: Dutch designer Piet Oudolf combines plants primarily on the basis of their form.

Bold and exotic plants need to be combined with less bold ones to add spice and drama to plantings that occasionally lapse into boredom. However wonderfully colorful a bank of shrubs might be in full flower, there will come a time when most of them will be past their best; a pampas grass in the middle of the winter will bring life and interest to a collection of such shrubs that have long since lost their leaves and had their last winter berry eaten by hungry birds. Likewise, a narrow bed of perennials and dwarf shrubs is difficult to keep going with flowers all summer; the dark and rather grand leaves of *Acanthus* (bear's breeches) will provide interest all summer, and its dead flower heads have a certain architectural interest right through until the beginning of winter.

PLANTING IN BORDERS

The border, which can take so many forms, is the home of the majority of the plants that we grow in our gardens. Combining plants to make an attractive spectacle for as much of the year as possible is surely the aim of every gardener, and bold plants have a special role to play here. Flowers tend to predominate in most borders, and since many flowering plants are chosen without reference to what they look like when they have ceased performing, it is not surprising that many borders carry a lot of visual "dead weight" for much of the year. Evergreens provide all-year interest, but they are not always that striking to look at. It is the role of bold and exotic plants to add a further element of continuity, structure, and interest to borders.

The kind of vertical lines provided by foxgloves and mulleins give a terrific lift for a border, and, more subtly, so do the tall canes of bamboos or the upright stems and flower spikes of *Veronicastrum virginicum*. Leaves that are larger than usual or have a particularly unusual shape provide a change of pace to flowers or smaller fussier leaves, an element of variation that is often not consciously noticed. Plants with linear foliage have a most important role to play here: irises, daylilies, and red hot pokers are the most widely grown linear-leaved plants, which are vital for creating a sense of variation. Since many irises are notoriously short blooming, it is good that they have this other virtue. Grasses, too, can add a linear element.

Taking a black-and-white photograph of a border will instantly highlight those plants that have structure, and many very colorful and highly thought of borders can look very boring when they lose

LEFT: *Verbascum* (mullein) are extremely usual plants in any border planting because they take up little ground space but they always add drama.

BELOW LEFT: The bold flower heads of *Salvia sclarea* var. *turkestanica* (clary sage) are a good contrast with the more subtle colouring and shapes of most perennials.

BOTTOM LEFT: **Lupins**, a classic cottage-garden flower, are particularly effective when planted in groups, soaring out from among other plants.

RIGHT: Linear leaves, especially those like the fine sword-shaped foliage of *Crocosmia* 'Lucifer', help to provide variation in the border.

BELOW RIGHT: The striking round heads of *Angelica archangelica*, one of the larger umbellifers, denote its relationship to the Queen Anne's lace.

their color. Try to accustom yourself to looking at plants and imagining that they are in monochrome—you will soon be able to pick out those that have definite structure, which may be because of the leaf shape, texture, and size; patterns of branching; overall shape; or the shape of flower heads. These are ones that will give structure to your borders, and it is the very best ones, the bold ones, that will, as a bonus, also add real character.

Using a particular kind of plant at random intervals creates a sense of rhythm and unity, and using a bold plant this way creates an even stronger sense of rhythm. The viewer will get the impression that here is a border that has been thought out and has been designed, not cobbled together from impulse purchases at the garden center.

But a word of caution: it is possible to overdo the use of bold and exotic plants. A linear-foliaged plant next to another quite often does not look right, while having too many strong shapes next to each other can also create a sense of fussiness, confusion, and over-excitement. Like all good things, bold and exotic plants can be used to excess.

ABOVE LEFT: *Euphorbia characias* (spurge) with its tall spires of cool gray and *Bergenia* (elephant's ears) with their leathery glossy leaves are among the few perennials that are effectively evergreen.

ABOVE RIGHT: *Euphorbia amygdaloides* is a robust early-flowering plant for light dry shade, but be careful if positioning it near water: it can poison fish.

BELOW TOP: *Aristolochia macrophylla* (Dutchman's pipe) can be used to clothe areas of bare wall in summer, and it adds a compelling feeling of lushness to the garden with its generous heart-shaped leaves.

BELOW BOTTOM: Not only does *Euphorbia mellifera* have elegant evergreen foliage, but it has scented flowers in late winter, too, earning it its common name of honey spurge.

OPPOSITE: Umbellifers, such as this *Angelica*, are valuable for their seed heads that stand erect through the winter, as well as being strong structural elements for the summer.

PLANTING FOR ALL SEASONS

Many of the best bold and exotic plants are evergreen, but relying on evergreens denies the seasonal change that is such an important part of anything natural. The annual cycle of the growth and death of plants is a vital part of the satisfaction many get from gardening.

Spring sees the rapid growth of new leaves and shoots. Large-growing perennials offer some of the most exciting examples of these; nothing can beat watching the enormous leaves of the giant rhubarb (*Gunnera manicata*) expanding from their buds, offering a glimpse into a primeval world. Ornamental rhubarbs (*Rheum*) are dramatic, too, their new, maroon-flushed foliage, deeply crinkled as it emerges from fat red buds, closely followed by spectacular flower spikes. By early summer, bold foliage plants will have expanded their leaves and be looking their very freshest, while most of the members of the umbellifer family will have started to send up their flowering stems. The herb lovage (*Levisticum officinale*) earns a place in the border for its very tall stems, while the more spectacular angelica (*A. archangelica* and *A.atropurpurea*) have by now sent up their six-foot flowering stems, accompanied by broad, much-divided leaves.

Shrubs and climbers that previously looked like nothing more than dead sticks have now burgeoned into leaf and are growing new shoots, aralia and the large-leaved hydrangeas (notably *H. aspera*) making the most spectacular transformation. Large-leaved climbers such as Dutchman's pipe (*Aristolochia macrophylla*) and Chinese goose-berry (*Actinidia deliciosa*) create a sense of lushness as they hang from arbors or walls.

Early summer is the prime time for flowers in most gardens, especially if shrub roses play any part. But many gardens begin to lose interest a little for the next few months after this, which makes the role of good form and foliage even more important. The vast silvery-gray cardoon (*Cynara cardunculus*), or its near relative the Scotch thistle (*Onopordum acanthium*), with a similar color scheme, can be invaluable at this time, as can ligularias, which up to mid summer have existed only as clumps of broad leaves. Now they are sending up yellow daisies on flower spikes in a variety of shapes: branched heads in the case of *L. dentata*, soaring spires in the case of *L. przewalskii*. The plume poppies (*Macleaya*) come into their best now too, their fawn-gray leaves and the soft heads of their tiny flowers continuing to look good until well into the autumn.

Late summer and autumn sees many grasses begin to emerge from their hitherto inconspicuous mounds of greenery, making them increasingly important structural elements in the garden, their flower and seed heads registering every breeze. Autumn

color begins to take over from flower color: *Hydrangea quercifolia* is one of the best bold-leaved plants in this respect, while perhaps the finest is the powerful vine *Vitis coignetiae*, whose large leaves turn a spectacular fiery orange.

During the depths of winter, it is often bold plants that provide any interest that the garden has to offer. The seed heads of larger grasses like *Miscanthus* are resplendent with low winter sunshine glancing off them, especially when they are rimed with frost, while perennials with dead stems that form strongly graphic shapes, like teasels (*Dipsacus fullonum*) or the giant hogweed (*Heracleum mantegazzianum*) are best when looming eerily out of winter mist.

OPPOSITE ABOVE: The large, hairy leaves of *Hydrangea aspera* relish the light shade and shelter offered by the side of a house wall.

ABOVE LEFT: A variety of different *Miscanthus* cultivars respond in unison to the breeze, creating a sea of movement in the garden.

ABOVE TOP RIGHT: The divided leaves of *Ligularia prezewalskii* add definition to a wetland planting.

ABOVE BOTTOM RIGHT: Sunlight shining through the vine sleaves of *Vitis coignetiae* shows off their delicate veining and highlights their stunning autumn color.

RIGHT: *Cyperus eragrostis* is one of those waterside plants that has enough structure to stand through the winter looking sculptural.

SHADE

Shade is often regarded as a difficult situation in which to garden. The range of plants that thrive is limited, and most of them tend to flower in the late winter to early summer period, with little after that. However, they make up for this by offering a wider range of foliage interest over a longer period than plants of open sunny places. Species that live in shade need to make the most of all the available light, so are more likely to be evergreen, with the attractively glossy quality foliage so many evergreens have. There is a very broad choice of foliage shapes and textures, too.

How a shaded area is to be planted depends very much on how deep the shade is and how moist and fertile the soil. Moisture and high fertility can, to some extent, make up for lack of light. Deep shade, especially if the soil is dry through the presence of tree roots or building foundations, is the most difficult situation of all, and there are very few species that will flourish in this challenging environment. Ivies are the most successful, but only the green-leaved, rather than the variegated ones, with the large-leaved *Hedera canariensis* making a change from the normal *H. helix*, which incidentally also has a vast number of forms to choose from. The glossy-leaved evergreen hart's-tongue fern, *Asplenium scolopendrium*, is also remarkably tolerant of deep shade.

Moist shade, or at least a situation where the soil never really dries out, offers the possibility to grow a wide range of first-class foliage plants. Ferns come in a variety of shapes and sizes, the larger ones, often species of *Dryopteris*, being useful because they are notably taller than the rather uniformly low level of most shade-dwelling plants. It is good to contrast the intricate nature of ferns with some large leaves, hostas being well established and popular for this kind of situation, and the ideal companion. But there are so many alternatives to hostas if you want more exotic leaves—*Arisaema*, for example, have mysterious arum-lilylike flowers in spring, and combine having broad leaves with interesting shapes, or *Podophyllym hexandrum*,

LEFT: *Helleborus foetidus* does remarkably well in dry shade, flowering in late winter. Its dark leaves look good all year round.

TOP: Hostas—these are *H. elata* and *H. sieboldiana*—flourish in moist shade. The *Aruncus dioicus* in the background is less fussy about moisture.

ABOVE: The leaves of *Podophyllum delavayi* are quite spectacular.

TOP RIGHT: *Matteuccia struthiopteris*, the shuttlecock fern, needs a moist site to do well.

CENTER RIGHT: *Dryopteris* ferns combine good overall form with attractive filigree foliage.

BOTTOM RIGHT: Glossy-leaved ivy, *Hedera canariensis*, is one of the most resilient shade-tolerant plants.

FAR RIGHT: *Dicentra* 'Stuart Boothman' (shown in rear) enjoys a shady spot with the fern *Blechnum chilense*.

with white spring flowers. Larger plants for average-to-moist shade include *Aruncus dioicus*, with pinnate leaves, and *Rodgersia*. The latter group, which include some of the finest bold-leaved garden plants, usually have deeply textured and often bronze-tinged leaves that are impressive in size and shape as well. If the shade is relatively light, ligularia will thrive in these conditions, too.

Although most shade lovers are herbaceous perennials, there are a few shrubs that do well, and most of them have splendid foliage: mahonias with their pinnate hollylike leaves and upright growth, the large-leaved hydrangeas such as *H. aspera*, and the glossy-leaved Japanese aralia, *Fatsia japonica*. Bamboos like some shade, too, farther enhancing the possibilities of the darker realms of the garden.

DRY PLACES

Some dry environments support a wide variety of
dramatic plants. Whether these are suitable for
your own garden depends very much on the
prevailing climate. Gardens on well-drained soil in
Mediterranean climates, where winters are mild
and summers hot and frequently dry, can support
a great many species from desert and semi-desert
climates: spiky rosette-forming succulents like
agaves and aloes, cacti, and African euphorbias,
which mimic the true cacti. These bold forms can
make a highly effective contrast with the typical
vegetation of the open ground in Mediterranean
habitats, which usually consists of low softly rounded hummocky bushes, with evergreen gray-tinged foliage, such as species of lavender and California liliac (*Ceanothus*).

In cooler climates, the bold plant choice for dry sites is a lot more restricted, as the
really dramatic species tend not to be hardy; at least they are not hardy in climates
where cold is accompanied by damp. The issue of successfully planting a dry situation
is also complicated by the fact that there are several groups of plants that look similar
to the growth form of many dry climate plants, but in fact are not especially drought
tolerant. The red hot pokers (*Kniphofia*) are a good example: with their rosettes of
foliage and spikes of flowers in fiery tones, they look as if they belong on a sun-baked
hillside, as do many of the thistlelike sea hollies (*Eryngium*). These plants help conjure
up the feeling of a sere landscape, but do not flourish in regular drought conditions.

The gardener with a sunny dry site in a temperate climate has a good range of lower
hummock-forming plants like rock rose (*Cistus*) and lavender cotton (*Santolina*) to
choose from, among which only a few bold plants will be needed to make an impact.
Yuccas are high-altitude semi-desert plants and thus remarkably tolerant of both cold
winters and drought, and can be used to great effect with their clump-forming spiky
rosettes, as can the dwarf fan palm (*Chamaerops humilis)*, if the site is warm enough,
while the 'Skyrocket' juniper can be dotted around to provide the romance and drama
evoked by the Italian cypress (*Cupressus sempervirens*). The latter incidentally is hardier
than often thought, and it will happily survive in most maritime-influenced
climates. As an alternative to the 'Skyrocket' if space is restricted, *Juniperus communis*
'Hibernica' is a smaller specimen and slower growing.

Bear's breeches (*Acanthus*), with deeply cut leaves and
distinctive flower spikes, does well on dry sites, and the seed
heads can be left on for winter, adding to a sense of drama.
Yellow asphodel (*Asphodeline lutea*) is similarly dramatic, its
tight spires best when several plants are grown together.

LEFT: *Gunnera manicata* (giant rhubarb) is undoubtedly the quintessential waterside plant, but this impressive plant needs a lot of space to allow its leaves to expand to their full extent.

BELOW: All ligularia are worth growing both for the fine quality of their foliage as well as their dramatic flower heads. The leaves of *L. wilsoniana* are jagged edged and crinkled with a purple tinge.

RIGHT: Ligularia will grow in average garden soil, but they look much better growing in the damp, as their foliage will be much lusher and their growth more luxuriant.

FAR RIGHT: Close inspection of the leaves of *Ligularia* 'Othello' often offers qualities that are not always appreciated from afar.

BELOW RIGHT: *Darmera peltata*, with its umbrella-shaped leaves that give it is common name of "umbrella plant", is an invaluable plant for helping to hold together loose mud, stabilizing the banks of ponds and rivers.

WET PLACES

Areas of the garden that experience waterlogging can be inimical to the growth of many garden plants. There are, however, many highly attractive plants native to wetland environments that will be only too happy to grow in your boggy patch or next to a pond or water feature where the soil is actually wet. Many of them feature large and dramatic foliage, as constant moisture can support the luxuriant growth that other habitats cannot. They can be grown in an artificial bog garden, where a pond liner, or thick plastic, is filled with earth to a depth of at least 18 inches, and then watered regularly. Such a bog garden can also be incorporated into a pond. Given the way that large-leaved plants grow, it would make sense to include a boggy area in a tropical planting *(see* The Tropical Look, *pages 60–61.)*

Large-leaved moisture-loving plants are often used as waterside planting, the leaves arching out at some distance over the surface of the water, helping to cast the shade that is so important for fish and other pond life. The classic plant for this situation is *Gunnera manicata*, the giant rhubarb, that seems almost inevitably to disport its vast leaves by the lakes of English country houses. A smaller, more manageable version is *G. tinctoria*, and alternatives for more domestic-sized bodies of water might be any

of the *Rheum* species (although they prefer to be moist, but not waterlogged) or *Rodgersia*, all of which have large, horizontally held leaves of great magnificence. Really wet places are suitable for *Darmera peltatum* (umbrella plant) with circular leaves supported by a stem in the middle. Its thick

rhizomes creep over the surface of mud, binding it together, which can be quite useful in situations where erosion or instability might be a problem. Apart from *Darmera*, which spreads fairly slowly, none of the plants mentioned so far are very invasive. Most *Petasites* are, however, which makes the huge *P. japonicus* var. *giganteus*, with round leaves to two feet wide, suitable only for large expanses of bank or wet ground. An established plant is a truly magnificent sight. The oval-leaved skunk cabbages (species of *Lysichiton*) are also fairly invasive in very wet conditions.

Reeds offer the perfect contrast to large-leaved perennials; their uprights balance the horizontals of the latter, and they provide an element of height. *Arundo donax* , the giant reed, is common in Mediterranean countries that does well in colder climates, growing to 10 feet, while its beautiful variegated form 'Versicolor' is unfortunately less hardy. Narrower-leaved alternatives include *Miscanthus floridulus* or *M. sacchariflorus,* which reach a similar height. More elegant than these are the cultivars of *M. sinensis,* which grow to around 6 feet ('Silberfeder' is the best known), and whose bold clumps

FAR LEFT: *Miscanthus* grasses, *Osmunda regalis* (royal fern) and other moisture-loving plants thrive in a bog garden.

CENTER LEFT: *Lysichiton camtschatcensis*, known as the skunk cabbage, is an exceptionally early-flowering waterside or marginal plant, with large leaves that reach their full glory later in the season.

LEFT: Big **grasses** and **ferns** appreciate a pond and bog garden made by making a hollow on low-lying ground.

BELOW FAR LEFT: *Lysichiton* 'Devonshire Cream' flowers in spring.

BELOW LEFT: The tree fern *Dicksonia antarctica* appreciates the humidity of a waterside situation.

ABOVE: *Iris pseudacorus* 'Variegata' provides a long season of interest either in the margins of water or on any site that never really dries out.

of leaves topped by silvery or pinkish plumes are remarkably elegant and evocative of reeds at their best. Note that they do not like being absolutely waterlogged. Species of reed-mace, or *Typha*, are good waterside or bog plants, but only if given a lot of space, while the common yellow flag iris, *I. pseudacorus*, has some of the largest and most striking foliage of any iris, being large and swordlike, an excellent contrast with horizontal foliage.

Many bog plants, but not all, seem happy in any ordinary garden conditions where the soil never dries out, but could not be described as moist. The foliage will never attain the magnificence achieved in wetter soils, though.

THE TROPICAL LOOK

The humid tropics are notable for the extravagance of their vegetation: huge leaves, vast swags of climbers hanging from trees, the prevalence of particular plant forms like palms and tree ferns. The feel of the tropics can be evoked quite successfully in cooler climates by using hardy plants with a similar growth form, and also by the judicious selection of plants that are on the borderline of hardiness.

Palms are the quintessential tropical plants, and given that *Trachycarpus fortunei*, the Chusan palm, is hardy to 4°, and that there are several other frost-tolerant species, a good beginning to an exotic garden is easy in any relatively sheltered yard. Bamboos also feature strongly in tropical environments, and so they are a must, especially those with broader foliage such as

TOP LEFT: The Chusan palm (*Trachycarpus fortunei*) is the hardiest widely available palm species, surviving temperatures well below freezing.

TOP RIGHT: Tall trees provide the shelter for an exotic understory planting of palms and tree ferns (*Dicksonia antarctica*). The shade cast is relatively light, allowing the plants on the ground to flourish.

LEFT: Chusan palms, along with some of the less hardy *Phoenix*, or date, palms transform a sheltered hillside.

ABOVE RIGHT: Spiky yuccas contrast with the elegant foliage of shrubby honey spurge, *Euphorbia mellifera*.

FAR RIGHT: **Cannas** are not particularly hardy, but they form an all-but-essential part of any temperate zone exotic planting. Some, like this cultivar, have the added bonus of a fine pattern of variegation.

species of *Indocalamus*. Tree ferns, which have a growth pattern superficially like that of palms, are only suitable for moist climates, since they absorb water through the trunk, and if temperatures never fall below 15° (the hardiest is *Dicksonia antarctica*).

Plants with very broad paddle-shaped leaves are also a part of many tropical scenes, kinds of banana especially. A few are root hardy, so if the stems can be protected against frost by wrapping with insulating material (*see* Temperature *pages 98–101*), they are a viable option. *Musa basjoo*, the hardy banana from Japan, has flourished in my sheltered city garden in the southwest of England for several years with this treatment. In colder climates, it would be possible to dig it up every autumn and bring into a solarium or greenhouse for protection. Cannas have a similar appeal, and since they die in winter anyway, they are much easier to either protect *in situ* with insulation or to dig up and store dry as tubers over the winter.

Sugarcane can be imitated by using the giant reed, *Arundo donax*, and the larger *Miscanthus* grasses, such as *M. sacchariflorus*, which thrive in any soil that does not regularly dry out. The spiky and rosette forming plants that are characteristic of many rain forests can be evoked by cordylines, which will eventually form a trunk, or where they are not hardy, yuccas.

Large-leaved climbers with thick woody stems ramble profusely over tropical trees, and there are several very hardy climbers that do just this in temperate climates, such as the vine *Vitis coignetiae* and the Chinese gooseberry, *Actinidia chinensis*. *Clematis armandii* is also hardy, and is invaluable in that it is one of very few evergreen climbers. Its glossy dark leaves can look very tropical indeed, and it grows vigorously enough to cover an expanse of wall. These larger-leaved exotic climbers can be encouraged to grow through larger trees, where their foliage will constantly appear and reappear among the branches, sometimes hanging down in equatorial-looking swags when they cannot make a footing on the branches themselves.

ABOVE: A Japanese banana,
Musa basjoo, is the centerpiece
of a planting of colorful
summer-flowering perennials

RIGHT: *Crocosmia* 'Lucifer' and
(left) daylilies (*Hemerocallis*)
are vibrant in midsummer.

BELOW: The castor oil plant,
Ricinus communis, is a fast-
growing annual that adds an
instant exotic touch to any
summer planting.

OPPOSITE: A variegated New
Zealand flax (*Phormium tenax*)
is a good permanent centerpiece
for a large area of tender
summer-flowering species.

SUMMER PLANTINGS

Using bold and exotic plants as focal points was a common practice in Victorian formal bedding plans, as we saw on pages 37–38. Those gardeners with conservatories may well want to consider setting out some of their container-grown plants during the warmer months, and it is possible to do this with many house plants as well.

In the Victorian tradition, bold plants were used as "dot plants"; they were spaced at regular intervals to contrast with much lower-growing bedding plants, which were arranged in strict geometrical patterns. The form and somber greens of the dot plants is a powerful contrast to the brilliant colors of the latter. The strong colors together

with the exotic shapes of the dot plants created a spectacle that was totally different from anything that would normally be found in a temperate-zone garden. Today's gardener, with limited space to store plants for the winter indoors, is most likely to rely on house plants such as *Dracaena* and *Schefflera*, cordylines, or cannas, which can be stored as tubers over the winter. Annual bold plants such as *Ricinus communis*, the castor oil plant, can be used this way.

Modern gardeners, though, are likely to see the geometry of the Victorian style as too restrictive and controlling. But it is possible to use a combination of colorful summer

OPPOSITE: Cannas are readily combined with other perennials or annuals. They are best planted in the garden every year and stored as dry tubers over winter in cold areas.

BELOW: The purple-flowered *Cynara cardunculus* is one of the boldest and most dramatic of perennials, creating a magnificent display over a long season.

RIGHT: The hardy banana (*Musa basjoo*), with the broad leaves of the empress tree (*Paulownia tomentosa*), add boldness to the garden in summer. They offer contrast to the tall sprays of purple flowers of *Verbena bonariensis*.

bedding and annuals with tender bold plants in a much softer way. A good example is the former rose garden of the controversial English garden writer Christopher Lloyd, who a few years ago dug up his traditional rose garden and replanted it with a mixture of exotic-looking bold plants, many of them house plants bedded out for the summer, and quick-growing flowering species. The colors are much more harmonious than the Victorian style and the overall effect more naturalistic.

The new generation of summer bedding, often referred to as "patio plants," such as *Diascia* (twinspur), *Penstemon* (beard tongue), and *Osteospermum* (African daisy), are far more lax and natural looking in growth than the older style of compact bedding plants, such as French marigolds, lobelia, and red salvias. They are easier to combine with plants that are not too rigidly symmetrical or formal in appearance. The silvery leaves of the magnificent *Melianthus major* (honey bush) combine well with the pinks and mauves of many of the new flowering plants, or the clean white of the giant reed, *Arundo donax* var. *versicolor*.

For those who do not have tender plants to bed out, but who are nevertheless attracted by the idea of creating a new and different planting plan every summer, it is possible to combine bold and exotic plants as permanent features in borders that are surrounded by planting that is to be renewed every year. Shrubs like *Fatsia japonica* (Japanese aralia) have the formal qualities of traditional dot plants, while perennials such as *Macleaya* (plume poppy) or *Cynara cardunculus* (cardoon) can be used if a less traditional look is desired.

CONTAINERS

Growing plants in containers is for some people— those with balconies or backyards with only a hard surface—the only way to garden. But container growing is also popular with many others too—those who like to dot plants around patio and terrace areas or like to combine plants with containers chosen for a particular artistic purpose, the classic cordyline in an urn being a good example of the latter. Containerized plants can also be used in a sort of subtle subterfuge in the border as well, if positioned among plants growing in the open ground, with the container concealed; a good way of instantly bringing some life to a rather jaded planting plan, perhaps, or of providing an instant or temporary effect. It is the sheer flexibility of container growing that makes it so popular; the ability to move fully grown plants around to exactly where they are needed.

Groups of plants in containers usually concentrate on cheerful summer-flowering plants such as *Pelargonium* (geranium) and *Diascia* (twinspur), which lack strong form. The addition of a bold plant, with large leaves or a definite shape, makes all the difference, providing structure and framework. Winter plantings, of bulbs, pansies, or primroses can work well with dark-leaved evergreens, exploiting the contrast between somber evergreen tones and the cheerful colors of the bedding.

The most popular bold plants for container growing are evergreens; plants valued for the continuity they bring to the garden. Examples include conifers or formal evergreen shrubs like Japanese aralia (*Fatsia japonica*), *Magnolia grandiflora*, or hollies, which can be used as the centerpiece of flowering plants in containers , or combined with looser-growing evergreen or deciduous foliage plants such as grasses, bergenias, or hellebores. Any evergreen bold plant in a pot can be moved into position to bring life and a sense of structure and order to anywhere temporarily lacking these qualities. Bamboos in containers have bulk, as well as a more informal elegance, while plants like New Zealand flax (*Phormium tenax*) and palms can hint at the exotic.

Deciduous plants have their uses in containers, although they are less popular, partly I suspect as they tend to be demanding of water. Hostas, though, especially larger-leaved cultivars, have long been used in containers, but there is no reason why ornamental rhubarb (*Rheum*), honey bush (*Melianthus major*), and ferns should not also be used. Many have distinctly colored leaves; the purple tones of *Rheum* or the silver of *Melianthus* can be used to set the theme for associated flowering or less bold foliage.

TOP: Pots containing tender *Abutilon* (flowering maple) and *Melianthus major* (honey bush) are arranged alongside an array of flowering annuals.

ABOVE LEFT: *Phormium tenax* (New Zealand flax) makes an attractive container plant, and this type of cultivation also restricts its growth—vital in small spaces.

ABOVE RIGHT: Keeping agaves and aloes in containers means they can easily be carried inside for the winter.

OPPOSITE: A selection of tender plants in containers can be easily taken indoors when frosts threaten. They can also be endlessly rearranged.

COURTYARDS

Courtyard plantings can present a variety of problems to gardeners, such as poor light and lack of space and soil in which to grow plants, although they do have the advantage of often providing very sheltered conditions. They can so easily be utterly transformed by the addition of some well-chosen greenery. Bold foliage plants are useful here for their long season of interest; in a confined space like this, it is vital that every plant earns its keep for as long as possible. As a source of inspiration, and for a harmonious selection of species chosen for the elegance of their leaves and stems, traditional Japanese courtyard gardens have much to offer.

Containers can be invaluable in courtyards, even making it possible to shift plants around so that they can alternate between comparative gloom and a position that offers more light but is less visually important. It is also possible to create raised beds where there is no open ground, using bricks, railroad ties, or other heavy support materials to enclose soil, which should be at least a foot deep, and have some drainage incorporated at the bottom.

The shaded and sheltered conditions of many courtyards mimic woodlands, so, if regular watering is assured, they are ideal for ferns, shade-lovering plants, ivies, and bamboos. The bamboos will be the most visually dominant element, and their canes can be contrasted with ivy grown as ground cover, or used as a climber running up adjacent walls; larger-leaved ivies such as *Hedera canariensis* do particularly well in sheltered places. Evergreen shade-tolerant plants such as *Helleborus foetidus* can be mixed in with deciduous ones such as hostas and ferns. For added seasonal color, flowering perennials like lungwort (*Pulmonaria*) or bulbs can also be added.

If there is an area of open ground to be planted, or if a deep enough raised bed can be created, then there are a number of shade-tolerant shrubs that have almost become courtyard classics. Japanese aralia (*Fatsia japonica*) is one, its big lobed leaves thriving in the absence of wind. The mahonias are another group of shrubs that do well in semi-shade, and the fact that they have an upright habit means they can fit into what might be a confined space. Most of them flower in the winter and have good scent, which is particularly appreciated in the vicinity of a door or window.

Large-leaved rhododendrons benefit from the shelter afforded by a courtyard, and grown in a raised bed, their need for a moisture-retaining, humus-rich acidic soil can be catered for. Grown with contrasting lighter green foliage of bamboos, a striking and elegant combination is made.

A sunny wall in a courtyard is a hot spot, making an ideal situation for borderline hardy plants such as the banana *Musa basjoo*, palms, or *Euphorbia mellifera* with its neat mound of fresh green leaves and whose flowers produce a rich honey scent in late winter that will be effectively trapped by the walls and thus perfume the entire area.

MODERN STYLE

An almost zenlike simplicity seems to be the hallmark of much contemporary style, and not surprisingly Japanese design has been a major inspiration for a great deal of the best in modern garden design. Bold and exotic plants have an important role to play in this kind of minimal planting—anything with small foliage simply seems to lack the sense of presence required to make an impact in a space where the hard landscape elements of stone, concrete, brick, glass, or metal are so dominant.

Contemporary architecture can often present a cold face to the world, lacking intimacy or human scale. One way to make it more amenable is by using plants, except that the plants are often overwhelmed and made to look irrelevant by the scale and the nature of the architecture. Only plants with large leaves or strong decisive shapes have enough character not to be thrust aside by the confidence of the buildings.

Plants with spiky leaves, such as flax (Phormium), yucca, and cordyline, have a restless dynamic quality that makes them eminently suitable for surroundings where there is a sense of looking to the future. They also have the strong shapes that make them stand out among the hard surfaces, and tough leathery leaves that resist the vicious vortices of wind that can play around modern buildings. The danger is, however, that these very useful plants are in danger of becoming clichés, as more developers and landscapers use them in commercial situations. Gardeners, who are able to devote more time and attention to their plantings, and to seek out plants that are less easily available, are in a better position to make interesting and novel collections of plants.

The key, I think, is effective contrast. The rosettes and swordlike leaves of yuccas need rounded shapes almost as an antidote, the two groups together almost a balance of ying and yang. Gunnera (giant rhubarb), Rheum (ornamental rhubarb), Rodgersia, and Ligularia all offer shapes that are almost an opposite. Most of these are, however, moisture-lovers and are most easily accommodated around a pond or in a bog garden of some kind. Less greedy of water, but also very effective, are the shrubby Fatsia japonica (Japanese aralia) or, among perennials, Crambe (seakale)or Macleaya (plume poppy). A formal repetition of particular bold or exotic plants can also be highly effective in modern surroundings.

Alternatively, the spiky shapes may be balanced by hard landscaping features, such as pebbles or stones. These, of course, emphasize the dry and desert feelings evoked by spiky-leaved plants, the two working together to produce a drily exotic ambience. I have also seen large glass bottles used as a contrast to these plants. Other containers made of metal or plastic could also be used.

ABOVE LEFT: Yuccas are extremely useful plants in that they are among the most cold-hardy of drought tolerant and exotic-looking plants.

ABOVE NEAR RIGHT: A young *Agave americana* 'Variegata' is complemented by a sculptural galvanized metal spiral.

ABOVE RIGHT: Spiky plants set off by pebbles always evoke the desert.

RIGHT: Phormium (flax) can be highly effective, but they do need a lot of space—this one might well overwhelm the decking path next to it after a couple more years' growth.

FAR RIGHT: Bamboo and steel—the formal repetition in the planting and the choice of modern materials make for a strong sense of contemporary minimalism.

ABOVE: If well managed, large plants in small spaces are highly effective, particularly if combined with water.

ABOVE RIGHT: Water provides context for lush tropical-looking plants, as well as an island of tranquility among busy visual stimulation.

RIGHT: A view out through a window into a garden crammed with large exotic plants to create a feeling of lushness is a look into another world.

FAR RIGHT: *Musa basjoo* (hardy banana) and *Arundo donax* (giant reed) thrive in a sheltered city garden, making the most of an urban microclimate. A flash of red is supplied by *Lobelia tupa*.

OPPOSITE RIGHT: A fig, *Ficus carica*, grows up a warm wall, making a feature of what otherwise might be dead space above a bench.

BIG PLANTS IN SMALL SPACES

Some are of the opinion that small gardens need small plants, others disagree. One of the latter is the highly successful American landscape designer James van Sweden, who says that "small plants only make a small space looker smaller still". I think he is right. Large plants in a small space extend the boundaries, pushing the vision upward and outward, creating the feeling that the garden and its owner are not limited by the physically limited space at their disposal. Big plants need not exclude smaller ones—there will usually

be room at their feet for smaller and more intricate specimens that will help to create an atmosphere of intimacy.

Tall bamboos, non- or slowly spreading ones such as *Semiarundinaria fatsuosa* or *Chusquea culeou*, are invaluable for giving a sense of height, while as a deciduous alternative a grass such as *Miscanthus floridulus* could be used. Large-leaved perennials such as *Rheum* (ornamental rhubarb), *Rodgersia*, or hostas can be used for the horizontal dimension. The giant rhubabrb, *Gunnera manicata*, might be just too big, but its smaller relative, *G. tinctoria*, may be a better fit. If the ground is moist, large-leaved plants will do much better.

Certain large or large-leaved plants can run invasively; bamboos are the most notorious for this, and the splendid perennial *Petasites japonicus* var. *giganteus* is one of the worst culprits. They can, however, be confined in planters, or by a solid surround to their growing area. Moisture-loving species like *Petasites* can also benefit from being grown in a container of some kind as it may help to keep it wetter, at least if there are no holes in the bottom.

Those trees and shrubs with larger-than-average leaves could be an exciting addition to a small garden, but their growth will have to be restricted. A happy side-effect of doing this is trees that are regularly coppiced, or cut back to the base to re-shoot, produce leaves up to 50 percent larger than normal. Pruned every few years *Paulownia tomentosa* (the empress tree) or *Ailanthus altissima* (the tree of heaven), are valuable additions. Other species with distinctive foliage, such as *Liriodendon tulipifera* (the tulip tree) or *Juglans regia* (walnut), can be treated in a similar way.

Large-leaved climbers are the final touch for small spaces. There might be space for them to ramble unhindered up a large expanse of wall or into a substantial tree, but most probably they will have to be kept strictly pruned, on a yearly basis, if the garden is not to be overrun.

THIS IS A SELECTION THAT AIMS
TO COVER AS MANY OF THE REALLY
GOOD BOLD-LEAVED AND EXOTIC
PLANTS AS POSSIBLE THAT ARE
HARDY IN COOL TEMPERATE
REGIONS, AS WELL AS A VERY FEW
THAT ARE NOT SO HARDY, BUT SO
SPECTACULAR THAT THEY ARE
WORTH MAKING A SPECIAL EFFORT
TO LOOK AFTER. THE FIGURES
GIVEN FOR HEIGHT (H) AND SPREAD
(S) INDICATE THE PLANT'S MAXIMUM
DIMENSIONS WHEN FULLY GROWN.

DIRECTORY

OPPOSITE: *Asplenium scolopendrium* is a fern that will thrive in very low light.

ABOVE: This detail shows the distinctive leaf markings of *Agave americana* 'Variegata.'

[1] *Acanthus mollis* (bear's breeches) is an adaptable Mediterranean perennial, often spreading in habit.

[2] *Actinidia chinensis* (Chinese gooseberry) is a vigorous climber that needs plenty of space to allow for free growth.

[3] *Aesculus angustifolia* (buckeye) combines good foliage and flowers, like all members of the genus.

[4] *Agave americana* 'Variegata' is one of many desert species among bold-leaved plants.

[5] *Aloe plicatilis* is not hardy, but worth protecting—aloes are an important group of desert plants.

ACANTHUS MOLLIS LATIFOLIUS GROUP

Handsome semi-evergreen perennials of statuesque habit, with long, oval, deeply cut, bright green leaves. Imposing spikes of murky mauve and white flowers in summer. Zones 7–9 H 4 feet x S 18 inches.

Cultivation: Fully hardy. Prefers sunny, warm conditions but will tolerate some shade. Deep roots may make it difficult to move. *A. mollis* can be invasive.

Uses: Ideal for mass planting with *Foeniculum vulgare* 'Purpureum' (fennel) or in a group against an old stone wall. Adds character when mixed with fine-leaved plants.

Alternatives: *A. spinosus* has more deeply divided leaves, a more refined appearance, and more colorful flowers. *A. dioscoridis* var. *perringii* is half the size and very fine.

ACTINIDIA DELICIOSA

(SYN. A.CHINENSIS)

Chinese gooseberry

A deciduous, fast-growing woody-stemmed climber. The heart-shaped leaves are 5—8 inches long with clusters of cup-shaped white flowers followed by edible, hairy, brown fruit.

Zones 7–9 H 35 feet.

Cultivation: To obtain fruits, grow male and female plants. Likes partial shade in any well-drained soil. Prune in winter if necessary.

Uses: Best against a wall or up a large tree or arbor.

Alternatives: *A. polygama* is less vigorous and self-fertile.

AESCULUS

Horse chestnut, buckeye

These deciduous trees or shrubs with palmate leaves (i.e. so deeply lobed that the segments are separate leaflets) have great character. Flowers are striking, arranged in "candles" in early summer. *A. hippocastaneum* is the most common, a large tree (H 50 feet x S 50 feet) with white flowers, *A. indica* and *A. californicum* are particularly fine, but smaller, with white flowers. *A.parviflora* is one of several large suckering shrubby species (H 13 feet x S 20 feet) with cream flowers. Zones 4–8 H 4–25m x S6–25m.

Cultivation: Any reasonable soil. Sun or light shade, with surprising tolerance of deeper shade.

Uses: All need space, but complement other trees or large shrubs well. Deep shade is cast by tree species, making it impossible to grow anything underneath. Shrubby species can be underplanted with drifts of perennials and bulbs.

AGAVE

Imposing succulents with sword-shaped, very sharp-toothed, evergreen leaves, spiked at the tip. They rarely flower. *A. americana* has gray-green fleshy leaves. *A.americana* 'Mediopicta' has a yellow stripe. Zones 9–11 H 3 feet x S 6 feet.

Cultivation: Full sun in well-drained soil. Bring inside in winter in frosty climates. Hardiness increases with age.

4

5

ALTERNATIVES: *Rhus* (sumac) species are less dramatic but smaller. *Pterocarya* (Chinese wingnut) have smaller leaves but a better overall shape and are fast growing.

ALOE

A huge group of succulents, with evergreen leaves in rosettes and generally orange flowers in spikes. *A. aristata* is a small species (H 4 inches x S 12 inches) with tight rosettes, *A. arborescens* is shrubby with long grayish leaves with spiny edges (H 6 feet x S 6 feet), *A. ferox* is a similar size and habit, but more aggressively spiny. All have orange tubular flowers on long spikes.
Zones 9–11 H 2 inches–13 feet x S12 inches–6 feet.
CULTIVATION: Survive only short overnight dry frosts, so suitable only for Mediterranean or other warm climates. Are very rewarding as garden plants in cooler climates if they are moved inside in winter. Some enthusiasts manage to grow them outside permanently in frosty climates if they are grown near stone walls, positioned to receive minimal rain. Good drainage and full sun are essential anywhere.
USES: Mediterranean or desert feel, with agaves, yuccas, etc. Good in containers as a focal point.
ALTERNATIVES: Agaves or yuccas.

ANGELICA

Handsome, large-leaved biennials, producing huge, deeply divided, leaves and umbels of white or green flowers in late summer. *A. archangelica* is the common variety, and the source of the herb. *A. atropurpurea* is dark leaved. *A.* 'Vicar's Mead' is smaller, with purple leaves.
Biennial H 6 feet x S 3 feet.
CULTIVATION: Save seed to start plants for future years. Sun or shade and in well-drained soil. Removing heads after flowering may prolong life.
USES: This is a dramatic border plant next to lower-growing plants. Good in small spaces to create a jungle effect. Combine with grasses, perennials and other large umbellifers.

ARALIA ELATA
Japanese angelica tree

Dramatic, almost palmlike, doubly pinnate leaves at the end of prickly stems, producing billowing heads of tiny white flower panicles in late summer, followed by bunches of dark berries. The deciduous form is bare and knobbly in winter. The cultivar *A. e.* 'Aureovariegata' has creamy-white margins to the leaves. Suckers to form imposing clumps.
Zones 4–9 H 10 feet x S 6 feet.
CULTIVATION: Prefers fertile, well-drained soil in sun or part shade with some shelter.
USES: Good with *Rheum palmatum* 'Atrosanguineum' (ornamental rhubarb).

ARALIA HERBACEOUS SPECIES

Very distinctive perennials with dramatic leaves, divided into leaflets and large ivylike panicles of creamy flowers in summer, often followed by dark berries. *A. cachemirica* has deeply cut pinnate leaves; *A. racemosa* and *A. californica* are roughly similar. *A. bipinnata* has striking doubly pinnate leaves.
Zones 4–9 H 5–6 feet x S 5–6 feet.
CULTIVATION: Sun or part-shade in fertile soil.
USES:: Good specimen plants in lawns, or in light shade with smaller perennials or shrubs. Striking when combined with bamboos.

USES: A strongly architectural plant that can be used as an exotic punctuation point in gravel planting, or highly effective in a pot. A mainstay of drought-tolerant Mediterranean or other warm climate plantings.
ALTERNATIVES: Yuccas. In frost-free climates some aloes are a less spiny possibility.

AILANTHUS ALTISSIMA
Tree of heaven

Fast-growing deciduous tree with pinnate leaves up to 24 inches long. Rather inconspicuous flowers.
Zones 4–9 H 65 feet x S 40 feet.
CULTIVATION: Needs shelter from wind. Any reasonable soil, but likes fertile deep ones. Sun.
USES: Specimen tree for large spaces. Can be pruned and grown among other large-leaved plants for exotic effect.

ARAUCARIA ARAUCANA
Monkey puzzle tree

One of the most striking of all trees. Thick dark green
evergreen leaves are on elegantly arranged branches.
Zones 4–9 H 65 feet x S 80 feet.
Cultivation: Any reasonable well-drained but moist soil.
Very windproof and thus good for coastal locations.
Uses: So distinctive that it tends to kill interest in
anything else around. Good specimen tree for a large
open space. Must not be crowded. Sets an exotic tone
for the rest of the garden.

ARISAEMA TRIPHYLLUM

One of many species, all with quality lobed leaves.
Curious arum-type flowers in spring. Dies down to tuber
over winter. Some hardy Far Eastern species, which may
eventually become commercially available, have huge
tropical-looking leaves on long stems.
Zones 4–8 H 18 inches x S 16 inches.
Cultivation: Moist but well-drained humus-rich woodland
soil, preferably slightly acid. Shade.
Uses: With other woodland plants like ferns, hellebores,
trilliums, etc.
Alternatives: *Arum* 'Pictum' is glossier, and has
interesting white veining, and it is more tolerant of
dry shade.

ARISTOLOCHIA MACROPHYLLA
Dutchman's pipe

Deciduous climber with large (10-inch wide) heart-
shaped leaves and odd spotted yellow flowers, giving the
plant its common name. Very vigorous.
Zones 4–8 H 35 feet.
Cultivation: Moist but well-drained soil, fertile, and rich in
organic matter. Sun, light shade.
Uses: Over large expanses of wall, substantial trees and
pergolas.
Alternatives: Other species may become available.
Actinidia deliciosa (Chinese gooseberry) is comparable.

ARUNCUS DIOICUS
(SYN. A. SYLVESTRIS)

A handsome erect perennial with large lance-shaped
leaves on tall stems and branching plumes of tiny
creamy-white flowers in summer.
Zones 3–9 H 6 feet x S 5 feet.
Cultivation: Thrives in well-drained soil and in sun
or light shade.
Uses: Splendid big plant in the white border next to
Crambe cordifolia (European seakale) or behind *Artemisia
lactiflora*. Also adds character to wild garden situations.
Alternatives: *Aruncus dioicus* 'Kneiffii' is a shorter form,
growing to H 3 feet x S 20 inches.

ARUNDO DONAX
Giant reed

Thick stems bear blue-green leaves and produce dense,
erect panicles of whitish-yellow spikes in summer.
Zones 6–10 H 20 feet x S 3 feet.
Cultivation: Slowly spreading grass, tolerant of part
shade and moist soil. In warmer climates may spread
aggressively in moisture. Tends to look messy over
winter in cool climates, so cut down to ground in spring.
Shelter appreciated.
Uses: Exotic near water and particularly good next to
Gunnera manicata (giant rhubarb).

1

2

3

4

ALTERNATIVES: *Arundo donax* var. *versicolor* (syn. *A.d.* 'Variegata') has broad creamy-white striped leaves; smaller and less hardy, but an exceptionally lovely foliage plant. *Miscanthus floridulus* and *M.sacchariflorus* are similar but much neater. Possibly hardier, too.

ASPLENIUM SCOLOPENDRIUM

Hart's tongue fern

Gains its common name from its bold leathery, bright green, tongue-shaped evergreen fronds that are banded beneath with spores.
Zones 3–8 H 18–30 inches x S 18 inches.
CULTIVATION: Likes shady, damp conditions and is tolerant if constantly splashed by cascading water. Good in alkaline soils and more tolerant of deep shade than any other ornamental.
USES: Dramatic in damp shady courtyards or basements with *Soleirolia soleirolii* (baby's tears) or in woodland planting with *Helleborus orientalis*.
ALTERNATIVES: Forms with wavy edged or divided fronds, such as *Asplenium scolopendrium* Marginatum Group.

ASTILBOIDES TABULARIS

(SYN. RODGERSIA TABULARIS)

Magnificent perennial with circular leaves that can be 3 feet across, supported by a stem in the middle of the leaf. Clusters of creamy flowers in summer.
Zones 5–7 H 3 feet (5 feet in flower) x S3 feet.
CULTIVATION: Moist, or wet soils. Sun or light shade.
USES: Consorts well with moisture-loving hostas, ligularia, *Rodgersia*, and grasses like *Miscanthus* and *Arundo*.
ALTERNATIVES: *Darmera peltata* (umbrella plant).

BERGENIA

Big-leaved *B. cordifolia* is an evergreen, clump-forming perennial with leathery glossy leaves and racemes of open cup-shaped, pink flowers in spring. *B. ciliata* is deciduous, with leaves 1 foot across, but needs shelter. *B. purpurascens* has narrower leaves that turn mahogany in winter if in full sun. There are lots of hybrids, too.
Zones 4–9 H 18 inches x S 24 inches.
CULTIVATION: Frost hardy, tolerant of sun or shade and any well-drained soil.
USES: Associates well with delicate ferns and the huge-leaved *Hosta* 'Halcyon.' Good in borders for winter/early season interest, or to top walls and raised beds.

BLECHNUM CHILENSE

A deciduous fern with coarse, primeval-looking fronds up to 20 inches long and a spreading habit.
Zones 10–11 H 20 inches x S 36 inches.
CULTIVATION: Hardy in milder climates, where temperatures rarely fall below 45°. Moist, not waterlogged ground. Shade, or sun if soil is moist enough.
USES: Splendid ground cover, alongside hostas, *Rodgersia*, *Rheum* (ornamental rhubarb).

CALAMAGROSTIS X ACUTIFLORA 'KARL FOERSTER'

Feather reed grass

Stiffly upright stems with tall bronze-purple flower spikes. Stands winter cold and winds very well. Deciduous
Zones 5–9 H 5–6 feet x S 3 feet.
CULTIVATION: Any reasonable soil in sun. Better with fertility and some moisture.
USES: Excellent focal point, or to create a feeling of reed bed or prairie. Group with lower-growing perennials or shrubs to show it off.
ALTERNATIVES: *C. x acutiflora* . 'Stricta' is almost identical.

[1] *Arisaema serratum* has weird flowers and good foliage for moist woodland situations.

[2] *Aristolochia macrophylla* (Dutchman's pipe) is a climber for a large expanse of warm wall.

[3] *Aruncus dioicus* has good foliage for light shade, with striking cream flowers.

[4] *Arundo donax* 'Variegata' (giant reed) is not hardy, but a most beautiful variegated plants.

[5] All *Bergenia* (elephant's ears) are invaluable for winter foliage and early flower.

[6] *Blechnum chilense* is a spectacular ground-covering fern for mild and moist conditions.

CANNA

Robust, showy, perennials with broad leaves tapering to a point. The flowers come in magnificent shades of yellow, orange, red, and pink. Some, like C. 'Wyoming', have rich dark foliage. C. iridiflora has particularly fine leaves and rich pink flowers. C. musifolia looks remarkably like a Musa species, i.e. a banana.
Zones 7–10 H 4–5 feet x S 30 inches.
Cultivation: Frost tender. Best to keep the rhizomes in greenhouse in pots of slightly damp soil or peat over the winter. Encourage into growth in spring under glass at a temperature of 60°. Plant out early summer.
Uses: Good in terracotta pots or in a mixed border with masses of summer flowers like Osteospermum (african daisy) or late-flowering perennials such as Crocosmia.

CAREX PENDULA
Weeping sedge

One of the largest sedges, with broad pleated semi-evergreen leaves. Long arching brown catkinlike flowers hang from elegantly arching stems in late spring, with seed heads remaining for the rest of the season.
Zones 5–9 H 3 feet (in flower) x S 3 feet.
Cultivation: Light shade with reasonable soil, but will tolerate dry shade. Can self-seed rather too generously.
Uses: Adds robust character to perennial plantings in shade, especially in wilder or coarser areas.
Alternatives: Many other sedges or species of Luzula have fine-quality evergreen leaves and thrive in similar conditions, but none have the same flowering habit.

CATALPA BIGNONIOIDES
Indian bean tree

Deciduous bright green leaves grow to 1 foot. Large clusters of white foxglovelike flowers in midsummer. In autumn these are replaced by long, drooping bunches of seed pods that remain for months and rattle in the wind.
Zones 6–9 H 30 feet x S 13 feet.
Cultivation: Plant in the dormant season in any soil type, dry or moist ground, but out of direct wind exposure.
Uses: The light green foliage looks stunning against a dark woodland backdrop and enhances a summer perennial bed of yellow and blue/violet shades.
Alternatives: C. b. 'Aurea' is an outstanding, slower-growing form with soft textured, golden-yellow leaves. Paulownia (empress tree) species have similarly exotic flowers and equally large leaves.

CHAMAEROPS HUMILIS
Dwarf fan palm

Shrubby clump-forming palm with spiky-looking fan-shaped leaves up to 24 inches wide.
Zones 7–9 H 13 feet x S 6 feet.
Cultivation: Hardy in milder climates only. Full sun and good drainage essential, especially if it is to survive regular frosts. Good as a sunny wall shrub.
Uses: Combine with yuccas and Mediterranean plants.
Alternatives: Young plants of Trachycarpus fortunei (Chusan palm) are similar and hardier.

CHUSQUEA CULEOU

Evergreen, non-running bamboo forming a dense clump of elegantly arching canes with leaves in bushy tufts.
Zones 6–9 H 13 feet x S 3 feet.
Cultivation: Moist but well-drained soil. Sun or light shade. Shelter.
Uses: Good for an oriental effect, or with smaller woodland evergreens. The best bamboo to grow as a specimen in a lawn or the centerpiece of a planting. The beautiful canes should not be obscured.
Alternatives: Other non-running small-leaved bamboos.

CLEMATIS ARMANDII

A strong-growing evergreen clematis, with glossy lance-shaped leaves of great refinement, bearing scented, flattish, single white flowers in early spring.
Zones 7–9 H 16 feet and possibly more.
Cultivation: Needs a wall or fence, sheltered from cold winds, and will require support. Remove any brown leaves and cut back if it outgrows its space. Could be grown through substantial trees, too, or be used to cover an arbor or tool shed.

ALTERNATIVES: *C. a* 'Atropurpurea' has purple to purplish-green leaves, but is more likely to need protection in winter. Yuccas are a very good hardier alternative to a small cordyline.

[1] Canna lily hybrids have rapidly growing exotic foliage followed by colorful flowers.

[2] *Carex pendula* (weeping sedge) is very easy and adaptable, thriving even in dry shade.

[3] *Catalpa bignonioides* (Indian bean tree) is long-lived and good looking from an early age.

[4] *Chusquea culeou* is one of the most sought-after non-running bamboos.

[5] *Cordyline australis* (New Zealand cabbage tree) is a striking plant that needs a mild climate to develop to its full potential.

USES: One of the best plants for a tropical ambience. Associates well with deciduous climbers or evergreens like the ivy *Hedera hibernica*, or as a backdrop to *Euphorbia characias* subsp. *wulfenii* for early season color.

CORDYLINE AUSTRALIS
New Zealand cabbage tree

Bold spiky shrub with broad-sword evergreen leaves of dull green with plumes of fragrant ivory flowers in spring.
Zones 9–10 H 3m x S 3m.
CULTIVATION: Best in fertile, well-drained soil, in full sun, hardy in milder climates. Can be grown in a pot to be carried indoors in winter in severe climates. Very successful in mild maritime climates where it shows considerable resistance to strong wind.
USES: Useful in a bed to give a spiky outline surrounded by dark-leaved *Hebe* or other evergreens. Good with bamboos and broad-leaved plants. Essential focal plant.

CORNUS CONTROVERSA
Giant dogwood

A handsome deciduous tree with tiered horizontal branches that look like a wedding cake, covered in late spring with tiny white flowers. In autumn the leaves turn to a rich shade of crimson and purple.
Zones 5–8 H 50 feet x S 50 feet.
CULTIVATION: Requires deep, fertile soil, neutral to acid in sun or part-shade.
USES: A rather special specimen tree underplanted with spring bulbs or hellebores. Must not be cramped.
ALTERNATIVES: *C. c.* 'Variegata' is a variegated. *Viburnum plicatum* 'Mariesii' (doublefile viburnum) is dumpier, but has a similar tiered habit and tolerates alkaline soils.

CORTADERIA SELLOANA

Evergreen clump-forming grass with dark green leaves. Huge white panicles of flower/seed on tall stems held well above the foliage. There are various variegated forms, usually smaller.
Zones 7–10 H 5 feet (8 feet in flower) x S 4 feet.
CULTIVATION: Any reasonable soil. Cut back in spring to tidy up. Full sun. Good in exposed situations.
USES: A magnificent plant that has become a cliché through overuse and planting in situations that are too small for it. Several clumps look wonderful in a large lawn or big open space. Otherwise combines well with large late-flowering perennials, like *Eupatorium purpureum*, or shrubs in beds. Often at its best in winter, accompanied by brightly colored-stemmed *Cornus* (dogwood) and *Salix* (willow) varieties.
ALTERNATIVES: *Miscanthus sinensis* cultivars offer much smaller and more refined plants that have a similarly long season.

CRAMBE CORDIFOLIA

European seakale

Large crinkled leathery leaves precede sprays of scented, white flowers that form a lasting display in early summer. After flowers have dropped, a skeletal form remains. Zones 6–9 H 6½ feet x S 4 feet.

CULTIVATION: Likes full sun but will tolerate some shade, any soil.

USES: A bold plant for the back of the border surrounded with old roses and *Verbena bonariensis*.

ALTERNATIVES: *C. maritima*, half the size, has the same qualities. *Rheum palmatum* (European seakale) will do well enough in most soils, but prefers more moisture.

CROCOSMIA 'LUCIFER'

Robust, clump-forming perennial with sword-shaped, erect, neatly pleated leaves and vermilion flowers in branching spikes in mid to late summer. Zones 5–9 H 3 feet x S 10 inches.

CULTIVATION: Prefers full sun and well-drained soil.

USES: Wonderful in large clumps with big red hot pokers, (*Kniphofia*) or lemon daylilies (*Hemerocallis*) or planted as specimen plant in a group on either side of an arch or gate. Will also grow in rough grass.

CUPRESSUS SEMPERVIRENS

Italian Cypress

The classic pencil-shaped tree of the Mediterranean, and very evocative. Dark evergreen foliage. Slow growing, with final height depending on climate. Zones 7–9 H 100 feet x S 6–10 feet.

CULTIVATION: Hardier than often thought, especially if protected in the first few years. Any well-drained soil in sun. Avoid frost hollows and sites with cold drying winds.

USES: Essential for creating a Mediterranean ambience. Mixes well with all other trees.

ALTERNATIVES: *C.s.* 'Green Spire' is a particularly narrow form with brighter green foliage. *Juniperus scopulorum* 'Skyrocket' is more suitable for cold climates and is smaller. *Juniperus communis* 'Hibernica' is smaller still.

CYNARA CARDUNCULUS

Cardoon

Large and dramatic perennial with jagged toothed silvery leaves and a big thistle like purple or blue head. Zones 6–8 H 5 feet x S 2½ feet

CULTIVATION: Any fertile soil in sun.

USES: With other silvers or brown foliage like *Euphorbia dulcis* 'Chameleon'.

ALTERNATIVES: *Onopordum acanthium* (Scotch thistle) is similar.

DARMERA PELTATA

Umbrella plant

Round leaves to 30 cms with big heads of dirty pink flowers emerging before the leaves in early spring. Spreading habit. Zones 6–8 H 2 feet x S 3 feet after 3 years.

CULTIVATION: Moist or wet soils, stream and pond sides. Sun or light shade.

USES: Combine with other large leaved waterside plants like *Rodgersia*.

ALTERNATIVES: *Astilboides tabularis*.

[1] *Crambe cordifolia* (European seakale) will retain an interesting form into winter if flower stems are not cut.

[2] The aptly named *Crocosmia* 'Lucifer' is pleasing both for its scarlet flowers and its fine foliage.

[3] The deeply-lobed foliage of *Cynara cardunculus* has a wonderfully jagged outline.

[4] The impressive leaves of *Darmera peltata* (umbrella plant) take on a reddish tinge in autumn.

[5] Blue-grey juvenile leaves on *Eucalyptus dalrympleana* give way to bright green adult leaves.

DICKSONIA ANTARCTICA
Tree fern

This deciduous fern resembles a palm with a tuft of fern leaves atop a dark hairy trunk.
Zones 9–11 H 13 feet x S 6½ feet.
CULTIVATION: Mild climates with frosts that do not go below 20° and high humidity all year are essential. Shade and moist but well-drained humus-rich soils.
USES: Exotic-looking climbers like *Actinidia* (Chinese gooseberry), other ferns, large-leaved shade-lovers. Essential for the primeval look.
ALTERNATIVES: Frost-free climates enjoy many tree fern.

DRYOPTERIS DILATATA

A handsome, semi-evergreen fern with much-divided, arching, mid-green fronds, with triangular divisions on thick, dark brown stems.
Zones 4–9 H 3 feet x S 18 inches.
CULTIVATION: Fully hardy, requires shade and moist soil, sheltered from wind and sun to keep the fronds in good condition. Regularly remove fading fronds to keep plant in peak condition.

USES: Good massed with *Pulmonaria* 'Ocupal' and *Bergenia cordifolia* 'Purpurea' for an interesting contrast of form and texture.
ALTERNATIVES: *Dryopteris erythrosora* is similar but smaller with new growth an interesting bronze colour. *D. filix-mas* is semi-evergreen and rather coarse but better in lighter conditions or where soil is somewhat dry. Many other larger ferns, e. g. *Polystichum* species.

ERYNGIUM GIGANTEUM
Miss Wilmott's Ghost

A biennial with spiky leaves and a stout thistly head in summer, drying to a ghostly winter form.
Zones 4–8 H 3 feet x S 1 foot
CULTIVATION: Usually self-seeds well in sun. Most soils. Great gravel garden plant.
USES: Adds great character to a perennial border. Best with lower growing plants or silver foliage.

ERYNGIUM PERENNIAL SPECIES
Sea holly

Many have greyish divided foliage and spiky flower heads. *Eryngium agavifolium* is one of the best, with a rosette of sword-shaped, sharply toothed leaves.
Zones 4–8 H 5 feet x S2 feet.
CULTIVATION: Any reasonable soil in sun. Most larger species resent drought. Those under 40cms when in flower, such as *E.bourgatii*, are drought tolerant.
USES: Good in the border with *Salvia nemorosa* hybrids and *Geranium psilostemon*. Add structure to perennial plantings and look good with umbellifers and grasses.

EUCALYPTUS

A huge group of evergreen trees from Australia with grey foliage, generally with quite different shaped leaves on younger and older trees, those on mature specimens being generally more elongated. With their gray bark and distinct open habit they are a striking group of trees. *Eucalyptus gunnii* and *E. niphophila* are generally reckoned to be the hardiest, but suitablility for different climatic conditions varies greatly within species; go to a specialized nursery who will advise you on what is best for your garden. If you can grow them, the species with the boldest leaves are *E. ficifolia* and *E. dalrympleana*; for areas that rarely experience severe winters.
Zones 4–9 H 70 feet x S 25 feet among larger species.
CULTIVATION: Full sun, most soils. Species must be chosen from areas with a similar climate to that which prevails at the planting site to ensure hardiness. Once planted they do not survive being transplanted. Fast growing but can be pruned to keep juvenile foliage.

USES: Often do not fit in with most temperate zone trees and shrubs. Look best with conifers and dry or exposed habitat plants such as *Phormium*, yuccas, heathers, and grasses.

4

5

EUPHORBIA LATHYRIS
Caper spurge

Very distinctive single stems with a rather severe arrangement of dark gray-green leaves. The sap is toxic, but it is meant to deter moles. Green flowers in summer. Biennial.
Zones 4–9 H 4 feet x S 1 foot.
Cultivation: Practically any soil in sun or light shade. Will always self-seed.
Uses: Adds a distinct, if slightly sinister, character to plantings of other short-lived plants like *Verbascum* species, or for mixing with true perennials. A good cottage garden plant.

EUPHORBIA MELLIFERA
Honey spurge

Velvet-textured, evergreen foliage with honey-scented, pinkish-brown flower heads, forming a rounded bush.
Zones 7–9 H 6 feet x S 6 feet (more in mild climates).
Cultivation: Most fertile soils in full sun. Tender and will require some shelter, ideally in front of a sunny wall.
Uses: An architectural plant effective with *Phormium tenax* (New Zealand flax).

FARGESIA MURELIAE

Bamboo with a clump-forming, non-running habit. Dense tufts of leaves and canes that age to yellow.
Zones 5–8 H 13 feet x S 3 feet.
Cultivation: Moist but well-drained soil. Sun or light shade. Shelter.
Uses: Good for an oriental effect, or with smaller woodland evergreens.
Alternatives: Other non-running bamboos.

FASCICULARIA PITCAIRNIFOLIA

A bromeliad (pineapple family) with rosettes of dark spiky-looking evergreen leaves hugging the ground. The center of the plant colours red when it flowers.
Zones 7—10 H 16 inches x S2 feet.
Cultivation: Milder areas with light frosts only. Does not like drought. Sun.
Uses: Looks good with eryngiums, succulents, yuccas, and rocks, even though it is not drought tolerant.
Alternatives: *F. bicolor* is not so common but more spectacular. Some *Eryngium*, e.g. *E. agavifolium*, have similar rosettes.

x FATSHEDERA LIZEI

An evergreen shrub, the result of a hybrid between common ivy, *Hedera helix*, and *Fatsia japonica* (Japanese aralia). A floppy shrub, it is best trained on a wall. Ivy-shaped leaves can grow up to 10 inches wide.
Zones 7–10 H 6 feet x S 10 feet.
Cultivation: Does best on fertile soils but fairly tolerant. Shade, including deep shade.
Uses: A good contrast to smaller-leaved and variegated ivies or to combine with other shade-tolerant plants like *Asplenium scolopendrium* or *Euphorbia robbiae*.
Alternatives: Large-leaved ivies like *Hedera canariensis*.

FATSIA JAPONICA
Japanese aralia

Evergreen rounded dense shrub. Sturdy shoots bear very large, deeply lobed glossy leaves. Clusters of creamy flowers in autumn are followed by rounded black fruits.

Zones 7–10 H 10 feet x S10 feet.
Cultivation: Most fertile, well-drained soils, shade or sun. Protection from wind important.
Uses: Effective with *Choisya ternata*, *Pseudosasa japonica* and *Euphorbia characias* subsp. *wulfenii*.

FERULA COMMUNIS
Giant fennel

Dramatic herbaceous umbellifer with large heads of yellow flowers above huge dissected leaves.
Zones 6–10 H 10 feet x S 3 feet.
Cultivation: Sunny well-drained position. Can take several years from seed. Not always reliably perennial.
Uses: Alongside other Mediterranean-climate plants.
Alternatives: *Molospermum peloponnesiacum* is another large umbellifer.

FICUS CARICA
Fig

Distinctive if slightly scruffy small tree. Characteristic large lobed leaves, insignificant flowers, and rounded fruit in autumn.
Zones 7–10 H13 feet x S 13 feet.
Cultivation: Any reasonable soil. Full sun. Often grown trained against a wall in cooler climates.
Uses: Good with other wall shrubs like *Ceanothus* (California lilac), adding a distinctive character. Small-flowered warmth-loving climbers like the herbaceous *Clematis texensis* or the winter-flowering *C. cirrhosa* can be trained through it.
Alternatives: *Fatsia japonica* (Japanese aralia) is hardier and evergreen.

[1] Naturally a small tree, *Euphorbia mellifera* (honey spurge) usually forms a shrub in gardens.

[2] *Fasicularia pitcairnifolia* is a low-growing hardy pineapple relative.

[3] *Fatsia japonica* (Japanese aralia) is surprisingly hardy if kept out of the wind.

[4] *Ferula communis* (giant fennel) is very tall umbellifer with finely divided dark foliage.

[5] *Griselina littoralis* has unique foliage with a richly glossy surface.

[6] *Gunnera manicata*—'rhubarb' that is only for the larger garden!

GRISELINIA LITTORALIS

A fast-growing evergreen shrub, densely packed with bright green leaves and tiny green-yellow flowers in late spring.
Zones 6–10 H 20 feet x S 16 feet.
Cultivation: Thrives in mild coastal areas in sun and fertile well-drained soil. Growth can be restricted with an early summer trim.
Uses: A fast hedge, excellent grown alone or mixed with *Prunus cerasifera* 'Nigra.'
Alternatives: *Griselina lucida* is similar, but has larger glossy dark green leaves.

GUNNERA MANICATA

Giant rhubarb

A vast architectural perennial with rounded, prickly-edged leaves, up to 5 feet across. Conical, light-green flower spikes in early summer are followed by orange-brown seed pods. Truly primeval.
Zones 7–10 H 6 feet x S 7 feet.
Cultivation: Requires a sheltered site; crowns may need protecting with a mulch in winter, in sun or part shade and in moist, fertile soil.
Uses: Excellent for watersides with other large-leaved plants like *Rodgersia* and *Rheum* (ornamental rhubarb).
Alternatives: *G.tinctoria* (syn. *G.chilensis*) is two-thirds the size. *Rheum* and *Rodgersia* are smaller.

HEDERA CANARIENSIS

Ivy

Handsome evergreen self-clinging climber with oval to triangular, unlobed glossy mid-green leaves on reddish-purple stems. In autumn, umbels of small, yellowish-green flowers are followed by globose black fruits.
Zones 8–10 H 20 feet x S 16 feet.
Cultivation: May be damaged in a severe winter but will recover in spring. Any reasonable soil.
Uses: Does well within the shelter of a wall and is tolerant of shade.

HEDYCHIUM GARDNERIANUM
Ginger lily

Perennial with vaguely maizelike foliage and big heads of pale orange scented flowers. Strongly spreading in suitable climates.
Zones 9–11 H 5 feet x S 2 feet.
ALTERNATIVES: Other smaller species are hardier.
CULTIVATION: Well-drained but moist soil in sun or light shade. Suitable for very mild climates only, although if insulated over the winter can be grown on a sunny wall in colder ones.
USES: Other large-leaved plants and bamboos.

HELLEBORUS ARGUTIFOLIUS

Mounds of remarkable gray-green three-parted leaves, with spiky edges. In late winter, pendant clusters of pale green flowers appear and last into spring.
Zones 6–8 H 30 inches x S 30 inches.
CULTIVATION: Enjoys part or full shade in deep rich soil. Will need protection from strong winds and scorching sun.
USES: Delightful in woodland setting with spring bulbs or in the border with bergenias

HELLEBORUS FOETIDUS

Evergreen perennial with divided, dark green leaves. Produces cup-shaped pale green flowers in late winter.
Zones 4–9 H 18 inches x S 18 inches.

CULTIVATION: Most fertile, well drained soils. Will tolerate shade and sun, including dry shade.
USES: Effective with *Lilium martagon* in summer, *Erythronium* and *Epimedium* in spring.

HERACLEUM MANTEGAZZIANUM
Giant hogweed

Most spectacular herbaceous plants. An umbellifer with huge divided leaves and enormous flower heads. Self-seeds alarmingly. Causes skin blistering in hot weather.
Biennial H 8 feet xS 4 feet.
CULTIVATION: Any fertile soil in sun or light shade. Dies after flowering but easily grown from seed.
USES: Combine with larger *Persicaria*, and large-leaved moisture-loving plants. Wonderful conversation piece.
ALTERNATIVES: *Heracleum lehmannianum* is smaller.

HOSTA SIEBOLDIANA VAR. 'ELEGANS'

A robust, clump-forming perennial with heart-shaped, ridged, blue-gray leaves. In summer, racemes of pale lilac, trumpet-shaped flowers appear above the foliage.
Zones 3–9 H 3 feet x S 5 feet.
CULTIVATION: Hostas decorate shady areas brilliantly, especially in rich, moist soils, but they also do well in sun if the soil is moist. Protect against slug damage.
USES: With bamboos and *Fatsia japonica* (Japanese aralia).
ALTERNATIVES: *Hosta* 'Halcyon' is similar.

HYDRANGEA ASPERA VILLOSA GROUP

A group of fine deciduous shrubs with lace-cap flowers composed of warm lilac flowerets, surrounded by paler larger flowerets, which appear in summer and autumn, and pointed, downy leaves. The habit is upright and suckering, looking gaunt in winter. *H. aspera subsp. sargentiana* has the largest leaves, to 10 inches long.
Zones 6–9 H 7 feet x S 8 feet.

[1] Evergreen **hellebores** have year-round appeal.

[2] *Helleborus foetidus* is the species with the best overall shape.

[3] *Heracleum lehmannianum* (giant hogweed) is a large and stylish umbellifer.

[4] *Hosta sieboldiana* has the best quilting pattern on its foliage.

[5] *Hydrangea quercifolia* has good autumn color and midsummer flowers that combine with an interesting leaf shape.

[6] *Iris japonica* builds up a mound of sword-shaped leaves.

CULTIVATION: Likes dappled shade away from winds and spring frosts. No pruning required. Dislikes dry soils.
USES: Where space allows, plant to glorious effect in groups underplanted with *Pulmonaria* 'Ocupol' (lungwort) or in front of a wall with *Vitis coignetiae*.

HYDRANGEA QUERCIFOLIA

A bushy, deciduous shrub, with deeply lobed, dark green leaves that turn red and purple in autumn. White flowers in midsummer to midautumn.
Zones 5–9 H 5 feet x S 8 feet.
CULTIVATION: Likes dappled shade, any soil. Good in humid summer climates.
USES: Good in naturalistic gardens, but useful as architectural plant in pairs to frame a gateway. Invaluable for late flowering and enhances a wall or fence of the ivy *Hedera helix* 'Goldheart.'

INDOCALAMUS LATIFOLIUS

Bamboo with exceptionally broad exotic-looking leaves on moderately spreading canes.
Zones 6–9 H 6 feet x S 3 feet.
CULTIVATION: Light shade in moist soil with a good humus content.
USES: Low-growing shade-lovers like *Pulmonaria* can be planted around the base.
ALTERNATIVES: *Sasa* species, although they are invasive.

IRIS FOETIDISSIMA

Magnificent orange seed-pods in autumn stand out against the evergreen, sword-shaped leaves and make up for the insignificant show of summer flowers. The leaves are aromatic when bruised, hence its popular name of roast-beef plant.
Zones 6–9 H 14 inches x S 16 inches.
CULTIVATION: Thrives in a bog or water garden but tolerates dry conditions in sun or part-shade.
USES: Good vertical leaf form that combine well with the spires of *Tellima grandiflora*.
ALTERNATIVES: *Iris unguicularis* (syn. *I. stylosa*) is evergreen, flowers in winter, and grows in very poor dry soil, such as near building foundations.

IRIS JAPONICA

Fans of broadly lance-shaped, glossy leaves and, in late spring, branched flower stems of flattish, frilled or ruffled, pale-lavender or white flowers marked violet around an orange crest.
Zones 7–9 H 32 inches x S indefinite.
CULTIVATION: Prefers the protection of a sheltered sunny wall in humus-rich moist soil.
USES: Good accent plant in a mixed border with *Euphorbia characias* subsp. *wulfenii* and *Hebe*.

JUNIPERUS SCOPULORUM 'SKYROCKET'

A distinctive evergreen conifer to create dramatic vertical form. Tall and columnar with a compact habit, and dense sprays of blue-gray foliage that pack the branches.
Zones 3–8 H 26 feet x S 30 inches.
CULTIVATION: Fully hardy and enjoys full sun in any soil.
USES: A striking focal point used either in pairs at an entrance or singly to define the end of a border.
ALTERNATIVES: *J. communis* 'Hibernica' is a smaller version. *Cupressus sempervirens* is taller, but not so hardy.

KALOPANAX SEPTEMLOBUS

(SYN. K. PICTUS, ELEUTHEROCOCCUS PICTUS)

A small deciduous tree with very neat, lobed, dark green foliage, to 12 inches across on young plants. Good yellow autumn color with small clusters of white flowers. Upright shape.

Zones 4–9 H 16 feet xS 13 feet.

CULTIVATION: Quite fast growing, especially on deep fertile soils. Prefers light shade. A good subject for coppicing.

USES: A good specimen plant, or will add character to a mixed or shrub border.

ALTERNATIVES: *K.s.* var. *maximowiczii* has more deeply cut foliage. x *Fastshedera lizei* has similar leaves but a less satisfactory habit.

KNIPHOFIA CAULESCENS

A stately upright, evergreen perennial with tufts of narrow, blue-green leaves and smooth, stout stems carrying spiky flowers of reddish-salmon in late summer or autumn.

Zones 6–9 H 3 feet x S 2 feet.

CULTIVATION: Requires a well-drained soil in the sun but tolerant of exposed, windy sites.

USES: Plant in large groups with *Miscanthus sinensis* 'Zebrinus' and *Macleaya cordata* (plume poppy) behind.

KNIPHOFIA: OTHER SPECIES AND CULTIVARS

Red hot poker

Most kniphofias are perennials with a rosette of gray-green leaves and bold orange or yellow flower heads in summer; useful plants for adding character to a border.

Zones 6–9 H 32 inches x S 20 inches.

CULTIVATION: Any reasonable soil in sun. Dislike drought.

USES: Flower heads add a vertical touch to borders, while the leaves are a good variation on most perennial foliage.

LEVISTICUM OFFICINALE

Lovage

Usually consigned to the herb garden, but a worthwhile plant for the border, with yellow umbelliferous flowers in summer on erect stems with distinctively cut foliage.

Zones 4–10 H 6 feet x S 28 inches.

CULTIVATION: Any reasonable soil in sun or part-shade.

USES: Primarily a culinary herb, lovage adds stature to the border, both because of its height and its chunkily cut leaves.

LIGULARIA

A striking perennial genus with large leaves and strong yellow daisy flowers in mid-summer. They lack subtlety, but are undeniably striking. *L. dentata* has rich dark-green heart-shaped leaves and orange-toned daisies. *L. stenocephala* has jaggedly triangular leaves leaves above which slender stems with dramatic spires of yellow flowers rise in mid to late summer, of which 'The Rocket' is superior. *L. japonica* has particularly deeply cut leaves but poor flowers. *L. stenocephala* has rounded leaves. *L. hodgsonii* is usefully smaller than most.

Zones 4–9 H 5 feet x S 4 feet.

CULTIVATION: Tolerant of sun or part-shade and wet conditions around ponds or in bog areas.

USES: Makes a powerful statement with other bold-leaved plants like *Rheum palmatum* (ornamental rhubarb).

LIRIODENDRON TULIPIFERA

Tulip tree

A deciduous tree, eventually very large, but can be kept pruned, when the very distinctive saddle-shaped leaves, which give it its common name, will be that much larger. Greenish-yellow flowers on older trees in early summer. Yellow autumn color.

Zones 5–9 H 100 feet x S 30 feet .

CULTIVATION: Prefers rich moist soils. Sun or light shade.

USES: Can be combined with other coppiced trees or used as a tree in a large garden, combining with most other species well.

LYSICHITON

Skunk cabbage

Distinctive bog perennials with huge undivided green leaves that appear after arum-shaped flowers in early spring. *L. americanus* is yellow and invasive.

[1] *Kniphofia* (red hot pokers) have striking flowers that rise above mounds of linear leaves.

[2] *Ligularia japonica* has the most heavily divided leaves among the genus.

[3] *Liriodendron tulipfera* (tulip tree) is a magnificent tree with unique saddle-shaped leaves.

[4] *Lysichiton americanus* (skunk cabbage) has huge leaves that follow the very early flowers.

[5] *Macleaya cordata* (plume poppy) is one of the best bold perennials for the smaller border.

[6] *Magnolia delavayi* has some of the largest leaves among the magnolias, and the white flowers appear over a very long season.

Cultivation: Sun and well-drained, but not dry, soil.
Uses: Good planted next to other large-leaved plants, the fine flowers adding a light touch, or with late-flowering, strongly colored flowers like *Aster* or *Monarda*.
Alternatives: *M. microcarpa* is very similar but can spread.

MAGNOLIA DELAVAYI

Evergreen tree or shrub with large oval leaves of deep blue-green above and bluish-white below. Slightly fragrant, bowl-shaped, parchment white flowers, open throughout summer into autumn.
Zones 7–9 H 35 feet x S 35 feet.
Cultivation: Requires sun or part-shade and protection from strong winds. Best in fertile, well-drained soil and tolerant of chalk.
Uses: Excellent as a specimen underplanted with hellebores and spring bulbs.

MAGNOLIA GRANDIFLORA

Evergreen rounded dense tree bearing large, bowl-shaped, very fragrant, white flowers from midsummer to autumn. The leaves are long, glossy, and mid to dark green with felty undersides.
Zones 7–9 H 35 feet x S 35 feet.
Cultivation: Requires sun or part-shade and protection from strong winds. Suits any soil and is drought-tolerant once established.
Uses: An excellent specimen plant underplanted with lilies and and hellebores. Often, however, grown trained as a wall shrub, where it forms a fine background for white flowers.

MAHONIA JAPONICA

A winter-flowering, evergreen shrub with bold leaves of hollylike leaflets and sprays of drooping, yellow flowers, similar to lily-of-the-valley in scent and form. Flowers from late autumn to spring.
Zones 6–8 H 10 feet x S 10 feet.
Cultivation: Tolerant of sun or part-shade in any soil and will thrive in damp conditions.
Uses: Good with other winter perennials like hellebores, bergenias, and *Iris foetidissima*, or evergreen ferns. Does well in courtyard plantings.
Alternatives: *M. x media* 'Charity' is very similar. *M. lomariifolia* has more elegant foliage, but is not so hardy. *Ilex* species of hollies are similar in overall appearance and also do well in shade.

Zones 5–9 H 3 feet x S 3–6 feet.
Cultivation: Wet soil, pond edges.
Uses: Combine with similarly large-leaved perennials like *Gunnera* (giant rhubarb), reeds like *Arundo*, and the smaller marginal perennials.

MACLEAYA CORDATA
Plume poppy

Bold, rounded, deeply lobed leaves, glaucous-gray above and white underneath, are held on stiff stems, that carry tall spires of masses of tiny ivory flowers in late summer.
Zones 4–9 H 5 feet x S2 feet.

MATTEUCCIA STRUTHIOPTERIS
Shuttlecock fern

Beautiful and graceful deciduous ferns with fresh green leaves in spring forming a shuttlecock shape.
Zones 2–9 H 32 inches x S 20 inches.
Cultivation: Shade or light shade and moisture – the more sun, the more water that is needed. Shelter from drying winds.
Uses: Other ferns, and moisture-loving perennials like hostas and *Rodgersia*.
Alternatives: *Dryopteris* and many other fern species.

MELIANTHUS MAJOR
Honey bush

Evergreen, oval-toothed blue-gray pinnate leaves and tubular brown flowers in spring/summer. One of the finest foliage plants.
Zones 9–10 H 10 feet x S 10 feet.
Cultivation: Not very hardy, so requires a sheltered position in sun and well-drained soil. If frost damaged, it will shoot again from the root. Best cut back in spring in any case.
Uses: Adds drama to a large pot under planted with Surfinia petunias. Good in a bed with *Verbena bonariensis*.
Alternatives: Gray-leaved forms of *Sanguisorba albiflora* (burnet) deserve the title of "poor man's *Melianthus*." Hardy but much smaller.

MISCANTHUS FLORIDULUS

Large deciduous grass that resemble sugarcane. Bright green strap-shaped leaves. Reedlike flowers in autumn but not regularly produced in cooler climates.
Zones 4–9 H 10 feet x S 3 feet.
Cultivation: Any reasonable soil in sun that does not dry out. Protect from wind.
Uses: Excellent with large-leaved plants like rheums. Can be used for screening.
Alternatives: *M.sacchariflorus* is similar but more likely to spread. *M. s.* 'Robustus' is a superior form. *Arundo donax* (giant reed) is similar but inferior.

MISCANTHUS SINENSIS

A grass that combines size with elegance. It has a great many cultivars with silver or ink-tinged flower/seed plumes in late summer and autumn, lasting well into winter, above clumps of green strap-shaped leaves, which generally have a paler midrib.
Zones 4–9 H 30 inches–10 feet x S 24 inches–36 inches.
Cultivation: Spreads and establishes slowly in any reasonable soil, preferably slightly moist. Sun.
Uses: Combine with large late-flowering perennials, smaller shrubs, other grasses. A fine complement to most bold-leaved plants.

MUSA BASJOO
Hardy bamboo

Spectacular hardy non-fruiting banana with 5-feet-big paddle-shaped leaves atop fleshy clump-forming trunks.
Zones 6–10 H 10 feet x S 3 feet.
Cultivation: Fertile, moist, well-drained soil. Shelter from strong wind vital. Wrap trunk in bubble plastic in winter.
Uses: Superb centrepiece for tropical-looking plants.
Alternatives: *Ensete ventricosum. Canna musifolia.*

ONOPORDUM ACANTHIUM
Scotch thistle

Bright silver-gray, thistlelike leaves. Branching flower stems bear deep purplish-pink flower heads in summer.
Biennial H 6 feet x S 3 feet.
Cultivation: Sun or part-shade in rich, well-drained soil. Tolerates dry conditions. Easily propagated by seed.
Uses: Adds drama and height to a wide border with silver-leaved plants like *Lychnis coronaria* and *Artemisia*. Striking with both pastel and strong-colored plants.

OSMUNDA REGALIS
Royal fern

An elegant and majestic deciduous fern producing bright green fronds in spring, pinkish when young, and turning to stunning rust and lemon tints in autumn. Mature plants produce rust-brown flowers.
Zones 4–9 H 6 feet x S 3 feet.

[1] *Matteuccia struthiopteris* (shuttlecock fern) is a moisture-loving fern with a distinct "vase" shape.

[2] *Miscanthus floridulus* 'Giganteus' is a large grass reminiscent of sugarcane.

[3] *Onopordum acanthium* (Scotch thistle) is a biennial with a dramatic flowering stem.

[4] *Osmunda regalis* (royal fern) is one of the most majestic ferns, usually grown as a waterside plant.

[5] *Petasites japonicus* is an aggressive groundcover plant with magnificently large leaves.

Cultivation: Fully hardy and tolerant of sun, but does best in very wet conditions in shade. Acid or neutral soil.
Uses: Excellent at the edge of water. Associates well with *Ligularia* and *Rodgersia*.

PAEONIA MLOKOSEWITSCHII

Perennial with soft bluish-green foliage, sometimes edged reddish-purple, followed by fat flower buds in spring that open to lemon-yellow, globular flowers. By midsummer, pods open to reveal shining black seeds nestling in a crimson lining.
Zones 5–8 H 30 inches x S 30 inches.
Cultivation: Prefers sun but tolerant of some shade and rich, well-drained soil.
Uses: Useful perennial for small spaces – the bold, architectural leaves create drama in enclosed spaces.
Alternatives: Many other *Paeonia*, especially the shrubby "tree peonies," have striking divided foliage, too.

PAULOWNIA TOMENTOSA
Empress tree

Deciduous, but can be grown as an herbaceous shrub in harsh climates. Large broad leaves, up to 40cms long and wide, especially on coppiced specimens. Large bunches of purple foxglove shaped flowers in late spring on older plants.
Zones 6–9 H 50 feet x S 23 feet.
Cultivation: Fertile, reasonably moist soils necessary for success.
Uses: A fine addition to borders of perennials or shrubs, the leaves making an effective contrast to smaller and more amorphous leaves and forms.
Alternatives: *Catalpa* (Indian bean tree) has smaller leaves but a similar effect, and is hardier.

PETASITES

Spreading perennials with heart-shaped leaves and erect clusters of fluffy flowers in early spring. *P.albus* is useful for difficult shade, while *P.japonicus* var. *giganteus* has huge leaves, up to 32 inches across, and a very invasive habit.
Zones 5–9 H 1 foot–3 feet x S 4 feet.
Cultivation: Sun or shade, moisture preferred.
Uses: Other large-leaved perennials and large robust grasses.
Alternatives: *Darmera* (umbrella plant), *Astilboides*.

[1] *Phormium tenax* (New Zealand flax) is an undeniably dramatic but unfortunately now much overused plant.

[2] The black stems of *Phyllostachys nigra* make this one of the most prized bamboos.

[3] *Pinus wallichiana* (Himalayan white pine) is one of several pines with bunches of long needles.

[4] *Podopyllum* species are part of a genus that thrives in moist shade.

[5] Where they can be grown, large-leaved rhododendrons are magnificent.

[6] An easy annual, *Ricinus communis* (castor oil plant) is traditionally used as a centerpiece in bedding plans.

[7] *Rodgersia* species all relish moist soil and will tolerate light shade.

PHORMIUM TENAX
New Zealand flax

A striking evergreen upright perennial with bold sword-shaped dark green leaves. Panicles of tubular red flowers on tall stems in summer. There are many cultivars with variegated foliage, which vary greatly in hardiness; it is essential you buy from a source that can give you advice. Zones 8–10 H 10 feet x S 6 feet.
Cultivation: Requires full sun and fertile well-drained soil. Best in mild climates.
Uses: Effective with *Euphorbia characias* subsp. *wulfenii* or *E.mellifera*. Good with massed *Sedum spectabile* in autumn, or hellebores in spring. Its bulk means it is an effective counterpoint to shrubs, evergreens especially. It is, however, in great danger of becoming a cliché through overuse by unimaginative landscape architects.

PHYLLOSTACHYS

A large group of bamboos, mostly with a moderately spreading habit. *P.nigra* is the famous black-stemmed bamboo, whil *P.aureosulcata* has yellow canes. Both are slow to spread. *P.bissetii* is elegant but more invasive. Zones 5–9 H10–13 feet x S 3–9 feet.
Cultivation: Moist well drained soil, protection from wind. Light shade.
Uses: Good courtyard plants. Mix well with low-growing woodland plants.

PINUS

The pines are one of the most ornamental tree groups. Most are large, but can be kept small if treated as semi-bonsai. *P.wallichiana* (Himalayan white pine) has spectacular long needles. Mexican species such as *P.patula* or *P.montezumae* have the largest needles. *P.radiata* is dramatic and makes a good windbreak. Zones 2–9 H 10–100 feet x S 13–40 feet.
Cultivation: Well-drained soil, including sandy. Full sun.
Uses: Work well with heathers, Mediterranean plants, and grasses or bamboos for an Oriental effect.

PODOCARPUS MACROPHYLLUS
Yew pine

Conifer with fleshy dark needles. Compact and unusual. Zones 8–10 H50 feet (in suitable climate) x S 20 feet.

Cultivation: Only suitable for milder climates, but successful as a container plant with winter protection. Tolerant of a wide range of soils, sun or light shade.
Uses: In Oriental-style courtyards or woodland. Good with bamboos, *Fatsia japonica* (Japanese aralia).
Alternatives: *Podocarpus salignus* is hardier with pendant willowlike leaves. *P.nivalis* is a hardy groundcovering shrub with distinctive foliage.

PODOPHYLLUM HEXANDRUM
(SYN. P. EMODI)

Glossy, deeply lobed leaves are mottled brownish-green, and almost hide the nodding white flowers, followed by fruits the size of plum tomatoes, shiny and red. Zones 6–10 H 15 inches x S12 inches.
Cultivation: Happiest in cool shade and in moist soil.
Uses: Excellent plants for the edge of woodland with cyclamen and ferns.

POPULUS LASIOCARPA

Oval deciduous leaves to 8 x 12 inches. Narrowly pyramidal tree, slower growing than most poplars. Zones 2–7 H 35 feet x S 25 feet
Cultivation: Any reasonable soil, sun or light shade.
Uses: Bamboos or larger shrubs.
Alternatives: *Paulownia* (tulip tree), *Catalpa* (Indian bean tree).

RHEUM PALMATUM 'BOWLES' CRIMSON'
Ornamental rhubarb

Handsome metallic purple leaves unfurl from dramatic crimson leaf buds. In late summer they fade to bronze on the upper surface and rich maroon beneath. Bright crimson-red flowers open in summer. Zones 5–9 H 6 feet x S 6 feet.
Cultivation: Needs moist, rich soil and plenty of space.
Uses: Good as specimen plant in groups with *Rodgersia* or *Gunnera manicata*. Adds structure to large borders.
Alternatives: *Rheum palmatum* 'Atropurpureum' has similar coloring but divided leaves. *R.* 'Ace of Hearts' has leaves that are green on the upper surface.

RICINUS COMMUNIS

Castor oil plant

An annual with large lobed rough-textured leaves and green and red flowers, followed by seed heads containing lethally toxic seeds.
Annual H 5 feet x S 6 feet.
CULTIVATION: Needs to be grown from seed in warmth indoors before planting out after any danger of frosts. Fertile soil, sun, and plenty of moisture needed.
USES: Very good for a tropical touch, with cannas, bananas, *Datura*, planted-out palms, or as a centerpiece with annuals.
ALTERNATIVES: *Fatsia japonica* is similar but hardy.

RODGERSIA AESCULIFOLIA

This handsome rhizomatous perennial has leaves like a horse chestnut, bronzed when the light catches them, and produces plumes of fragrant, pinkish-white flowers in summer. There are several similar species.
Zones 5–6 H 4 feet (when in flower) x S 3 feet.
CULTIVATION: Needs damp conditions, good on clay soils. Light shade is preferred.
USES: Excellent for planting near watersides where it forms huge clumps and looks striking next to round-leafed *Gunnera* or other large moisture-loving perennials and grasses.
ALTERNATIVES: *Astilboides* or *Darmera* (umbrella plant). *Gunnera tinctoria* where there is space.

RHODODENDRON: LARGE-LEAVED SPECIES

These are some of the largest leaved of all hardy shrubs. *R. sinogrande* is the most dramatic of many, with leaves to 12 x 36 inches. Evergreen, with dark glossy foliage.
Zones 8–9 H 30 feet x S 16 feet slowly.
CULTIVATION: Must have shelter, protection from severe frosts, an acid soil, and adequate moisture.
USES: Bamboos and magnolias for an exotic planting in the larger garden.

RUBUS PARVIFLORUS

Large vinelike hairy deciduous leaves on arching stems, with large white flowers in summer and red fruits.
Zones 6–9 H 6 feet x S 10 feet
CULTIVATION: Any reasonable soil, preferably light. Sun or part shade.
USES: Given its spreading habit, only realistic as a good high-level groundcover among large shrubs or trees.
ALTERNATIVES: *R.odoratus* is similar but potentially very invasive and with bright pink flowers.

SALIX MAGNIFICA
Willow

Magnolia-like deciduous leaves, up to 8 inches long. Slow growing. Yellow catkins.
Zones 2–8 H 13 feet x S 10 feet.
Cultivation: Any reasonable soil. Sun or light shade.
Uses: Stands out among other moisture-loving plants.
Alternatives: *S.fargesii* has similarly large leaves with distinctively glossy stems and red winter buds. Also slow.

SALVIA SCLAREA VAR. TURKESTANICA HORT.
Clary sage

In its second summer produces a spike of bluish flowers in distinctive mauve bracts over several weeks. Large hairy leaves. Lacks refinement but rather special.
Biennial H 3 feet x S 20 inches.
Cultivation: Any reasonable soil, and dry ones. Full sun. Cannot be relied upon to self-seed so save some seed to keep it going.
Uses: Perfect to add some large-leaved weight to wispy pink and blue flowers in pastel color schemes. Looks good with silver foliage.

SANGUISORBA
Burnet

Perennials with elegant pinnate leaves. Bobblelike flowers on tall stems in mid summer. *S.canadensis* and *S.tenuifolia* are most common; *S.parviflora* the most striking.
Zones 4–8 H 5 feet x S 2 feet.
Cultivation: Any reasonable soil that is not too dry. Like moisture, sun.
Uses: Add a touch of style to perennial borders.

SILPHIUM

Perennials with very thick large leaves. Yellow daisy flowers in late summer. *S.laciniatum* is the best, with extraordinary cut leaves.
Zones 4–10 H 10 feet (when flowering) x S 2 feet.
Cultivation: Any reasonable soil. Sun. Dislike disturbance.
Uses: Prairie or wilder border plantings.

TETRAPANAX PAPYRIFER

Source of rice paper. Large lobed rough-looking leaves—very exotic. Shrubby habit.
Zones 9–11 H 10 feet x S 10 feet.
Cultivation: Not reliably hardy. Can be treated as herbaceous. Needs fertile moist soil and shelter. Sun or part shade.
Uses: For an exotic effect alongside bamboos or smaller foliage grasses.
Alternatives: *Fatsia japonica* (Japanese aralia).

TRACHYCARPUS FORTUNEI
Chusan palm

An exotic evergreen palm with a head of large, deeply divided, fanlike mid-green leaves. In early summer, large sprays of fragrant cream flowers appear on mature plants.
Zones 7–10 H 35 feet x S 10 feet given plenty of time.
Cultivation: Frost hardy, to 5°, but does best in a position sheltered from strong winds and full sun or light shade. Does well in containers.
Uses: The architectural form adds drama even to a small garden and it is particularly good reflected in water, so waterside planting is recommended.

VERATRUM

Perennials with immensely superior pleated leaves on erect stems. *V.nigrum* has brown flowers in spikes in early summer, *V.album* off-white flowers.
Zones 3–8 H 5 feet x S 1 foot.
Cultivation: Well-drained moist soils. Can be slow. Sun or part shade.
Uses: Adds stature to more amorphous perennials.

[1] *Salvia sclarens* var. 'Turkestanica' (clary sage) is a biennial with large hairy leaves and a distinct resinous smell.

[2] *Sanguisorba officinalis* 'Tanna' (burnet) has dark red bobbles in midsummer and a long season of fine leaves.

[3] The finely pleated leaves of *Veratrum* are the characteristic that makes this species so distinctive.

[4] *Verbascum phlomoides* (mullein) is invaluable for height; mulleins usually self-seed easily, providing a ready supply of new plants.

[5] *Viburnum rhytidophyllum* (leatherleaf viburnum) has evergreen foliage with an unusual velvety texture.

[6] *Vitis coignetiae* was a classic subject for traditional Japanese planting and painting.

VIBURNUM RHYTIDOPHYLLUM
Leatherleaf viburnum

A handsome evergreen shrub with long narrow deep green rough-textured leaves and dense heads of creamy-white flower heads in summer, followed by red fruits that mature to black in early autumn.
Zones 5–9 H 10 feet x S 10 feet.
Cultivation: Enjoys sun or semi-shade in any fertile soil.
Uses: An excellent shrub to link a formal garden to a wilder part of the landscape, perhaps a small woodland.

VITIS COIGNETIAE

A vigorous ornamental vine with heart-shaped leaves measuring up to a foot across, turning spectacular purple-crimson in the autumn. Produces tiny pale green flowers in summer followed by black berries.
Zones 5–9 H 50 feet.
Cultivation: Requires a well drained humus-rich soil and does best in full sun but will tolerate some shade.
Uses: Effective growing against a stone wall or up into a large tree. Good background for other large-leaved plants or large grasses and late-flowering perennials.

YUCCA

Distinctive plants with rosettes of (sometimes dangerously) spiky evergreen leaves. Huge panicles of creamy flowers are produced after some years. Clump-forming. *Y. filamentosa*, *Y. flaccida*, and *Y. glauca* are very hardy varieties. The latter, and *Y. gloriosa*, produce a short trunk.
Zones 4–10 H 10 feet x S 10 feet.
Cultivation: Full sun, dry soil.
Uses: Invaluable for evoking a desert scene.
Alternatives: Agaves and aloes in warmer climates. Cordylines are vaguely similar, but much less spiky and less tolerant.

ZEA MAYS
Maize

Annual grass with broad leaves, as useful in the border as in the vegetable garden. Ornamental kinds produce corn that can be dried and used in indoor flower arrangements.
Annual H 6 feet x S16 feet.
Cultivation: Sow in fertile soil in sun when weather warms up in late spring.
Uses: As a structural element with other annuals or among large-leaved exotica.

VERBASCUM
Mullein

A large genus of short-lived perennials or biennials, many with strikingly tall flower spikes, nearly all with yellow flowers. Some form huge rosettes of semi-evergreen gray wooly leaves in the winter. *V. olympicum* and *V. bombyciferum* are the most effective.
Zones 5–9 H 6–16 feet x S 2 feet.
Cultivation: Any reasonable, or dry, soil in sun. Usually self-seed, sometimes rather too generously, after parent plants flower and die.
Uses: A border with a scattering of self-sown mulleins is magnificent, the yellow verticals giving it a strong sense of rhythm and unity. Combine well with most perennials.
Alternatives: *Digitalis* (foxglove), especially narrow-spiked *D. ferruginea*.

WHILE MOST BOLD AND EXOTIC
PLANTS ARE EASY, MANY COME
FROM AREAS WITH A DIFFERENT
CLIMATE FROM THAT IN YOUR
GARDEN. UNDERSTANDING YOUR
PREVAILING CONDITIONS IS THE
FIRST STEP TO CHOOSING PLANTS
THAT WILL SUCCEED. IN THIS
SECTION, WE CONSIDER MATCHING
PLANTS WITH THE ENVIRONMENT
AND LOOK AT HOW TO GET THE
BEST FROM THEM IN SITUATIONS
THAT ARE LESS THAN PERFECT.

PRACTICALITIES

OPPOSITE: The fronds of *Matteuccia struthiopteris*, the shuttlecock fern, emerge.

ABOVE: *Trachycarpus fortunei*, the Chusan palm, has very distinctive foliage.

BELOW: A *Phormium* and *Euphorbia mellifera* (honey spurge), among others, make the most of a spot sheltered from wind and extremes of temperature. Matching plants to their environment in this way will help you make sure your plants will not have to struggle to overcome adverse growing conditions.

OPPOSITE: The fresh young buds of *Paeonia* 'Coral Sunset' are a reminder that many plants are grown primarily for their foliage because that foliage has its own special value—in this case, the distinctive coloring and form of the young growth.

CHOOSING AND SITING BOLD AND EXOTIC PLANTS

Crucial to success with the cultivation of bold and exotic plants is choosing and siting them appropriately. Many originate in warmer climates than in our gardens, so we grow them at the very borderline of their range. However, there is huge variation in how hardy plants are within a small area, because of the microclimate. Features such as hills and valleys, along with walls, fences, trees, and slope, cause considerable differences in what weather is actually experienced.

If you are lucky, there will be a garden open to the public in your vicinity with a range of borderline plants; this will tell you what can be grown, but not necessarily what cannot. Gardeners today are more likely to experiment with plants and find to their surprise that certain plants will flourish where they are meant not to.

TEMPERATURE

Knowing the minimum temperature at which a plant may be grown can be misleading. Many cacti can withstand freezing, but only in desiccated desert air, and only overnight. There is a huge difference between the short dry frosts of the Mediterranean, the longer wet ones of maritime climates, or the even longer but dry frosts of continental ones. Gardens at higher altitudes and latitudes are liable to greater cold than lower ones. Warm sea currents make it possible to grow exotics on coasts that are impossible inland. Maritime climates, such as the Pacific Northwest, or the northwest of Europe, are milder, but more unpredictable—plants from continental climates may start to grow in a warm spell in spring, only to be badly damaged by late frosts they are not used to. Maritime climates offer long but not very warm growing seasons, whereas continental ones have short, but warmer, more intense seasons.

Understanding where a plant is from makes all the difference between success and failure. Roughly, plants experience two kinds of cold: wet and dry. For example, if a plant has spiky or succulent, or perhaps gray or silver leaves, this suggests it is from a seasonally dry climate, so it is intolerant of wet cold. If it is to survive in your garden, it will need very good drainage.

Plants often show localized genetic variation in how they react to cold. If plants are descendants of seed from a warm lowland valley, then the species will have a reputation for lack of hardiness that ignores the fact there are also strains that thrive on mountainsides and survive greater cold. Specialized nurseries often have plants from more than one origin and will know the differences between clones or particular local forms.

The microclimate of the planting position is crucial. South-facing walls in the Northern Hemisphere and north-facing ones in the Southern Hemisphere absorb more of the sun's rays, and are warmer. They absorb and radiate heat, so they function as storage heaters in the winter, keeping plants warm, and are hotter in summer, so woody plants ripen better, itself a major factor in enhancing winter survival. Cold air is heavy and sinks, which is why valley bottoms sometimes become frost hollows and why slopes offer better frost protection than flat land. Walls and other solid objects can dam up cold air on slopes, creating localized mini-frost hollows.

WIND

Some bold and exotic plants are frost hardy but wind tender; others the reverse. Those from sheltered, often wooded, environments in continental climates, such as *Fatsia japonica* (Japanese aralia) or the bamboos, will

tolerate deep frost, but not even moderate winds. This is true of many plants with large leaves. Then there are those that cannot survive cold but resist strong winds, such as *Griselinia littoralis*, with its small leathery leaves.

In fact, we need to distinguish between two kinds of winds: cold winds, and very strong but mild ones. The former add "wind chill factor" to cold air itself and add considerably to the harm frost causes. The latter are much gustier, and in places carry salt from the ocean, but the air is relatively warm, which is why many plants with leathery or gray leaves from Mediterranean or warm maritime climates can survive a good gale.

Most cold or strong winds occur outside the main growing season, so deciduous plants are at less risk than evergreens, which are severely damaged by cold winds. Indeed, there are few evergreens in this book that will flourish in sites that are exposed to cold winter winds.

Protection from wind is probably the vital factor in success with bold plants. Walls offer protection, but can cause damaging areas of turbulence, whereas hedges and fences with some gaps serve to break it up and weaken it more effectively. Growing wind-tender plants between buttresses of larger and tougher species is an old and trusted technique.

SOIL CONDITION AND TYPE

We have seen how bold and exotic plants are typically species of very dry or very wet habitats; their foliage is an adaptation to environment. Plants of dry places do not need to be grown in dry sites in the garden, but they must have good drainage; waterlogging, especially in winter, is often fatal. Plants of wet habitats often do well in ordinary soils, as long as they never dry out, but they rarely look as magnificent as in moister ones.

Drought-tolerant plants are more likely to do well on thin and poor soils; moisture-lovers respond to deeper and more fertile soils. Only a few bold and exotic plants, notably the rhododendrons, are intolerant of lime.

MANAGING TENDER PLANTS

It is a one of the characteristics of gardeners that we always strive for something that is just beyond what is regarded as possible. This urge is a strong factor behind the considerable current interest in growing plants that are only on the borderline of being hardy. And for those gardeners interested in exotic plants in particular, the desire is deepened by the fact that many of the most exciting exotic plants fall into this category.

There are two approaches to protecting borderline hardy plants in winter: one is to leave *in situ* and provide protection, the other is to bring inside. The first is less trouble, better for the plant in the long term, but more risky. It is suited to plants that are reasonably tough and need protection from only the worst winter ravages.

Woody plants or evergreen perennials such as agaves or phormiums with top-growth that needs protection are more difficult than herbaceous plants, as they need some kind of structure. Those grown against walls can be covered with bubble plastic or opaque organic material such as conifer branches or straw mats leaned against the wall, which will keep out several degrees of frost. Plastic lets in light, but encourages humidity and therefore the risk of damaging fungus diseases. If cold spells are likely to be of short duration, though, covers can be used as and when, which greatly limits any damage the plants may suffer through lack of light and air.

Bubble plastic is probably the easiest material to wrap trunks in, along with the leaves of plants which can be easily bundled together, such as cordylines and palms, but I would advise periodic inspections to assess whether fungal disease is causing problems, especially in mild weather. Cut all the leaves of banana (*Musa basjoo*) off near the trunk, leaving some bases to protect the growth point inside the trunk, before wrapping it in layers of plastic. Herbaceous plants such as cannas and *Gunnera* (the latter needs it in severe cold only) can be protected with straw held down by wire, pine needles covered in permeable sacking or any other organic material that traps air and will not become soggy. Slugs can be a problem under any sort of close cover.

An alternative to close covers is a cloche. You can assess what is going on underneath much better, but they (and plastic of any kind) should be removed once the danger of frosts of 26° or 28° are past as a "greenhouse" effect will encourage premature growth.

Container-grown plants can simply be picked up and carried into any indoor situation where they will receive some light. If the conditions are kept to a minimum of just above freezing and not raised too much on warm days, the plants' metabolism will be reduced, allowing them to survive in poor light. But a warm greenhouse or solarium will inevitably result in premature spring growth that will suffer in cooler outdoor temperatures if the plant is placed outside again too early. Plants dug up from the open ground in the border should also be put in pots and kept in similar conditions.

OPPOSITE: Too many strappy-leaved plants together can be fussy, but some gardeners like the exotic effect that results. *Phormium* dominate this scheme, with a **yucca** and others. Combining plants that have similar natural habitats makes it easier to make sure they receive optimum care.

SOIL PREPARATION AND PLANTING

If the plants chosen are appropriate to the conditions prevailing at the site, extensive soil modification will not be necessary. The one area where this may not hold is in the vicinity of buildings where human disturbance has resulted in large quantities of rubble being mixed into the soil, or where the topsoil has been removed. Yuccas and other plants of dry soils may not object too much, but most plants will do much better if large quantities of well-rotted manure, garden compost, or other decayed organic matter is dug in, to begin to build up the humus that is the core of a healthy soil. Slow-release organic fertilizers, derived from manure or seaweed, can also be applied to provide fertility. This kind of soil improvement is particularly important for shade-loving plants in situations where the soil is poor, —at the foot of walls, for example, or underneath trees if there is no layer of leaf mold. Woodland plants will only establish and flourish if they have a root run in a moisture-retaining humus-rich layer of topsoil.

When you are planting in normal unimproved soil, it is unnecessary, and may actually be harmful, to add compost or fertilizer. What does help, though, is to break up the soil at the base and around the sides of the planting hole, especially for woody plants. This helps their roots to penetrate the soil more quickly and seek water and nutrients effectively. When planting into clay soils from pots that have been filled with lightweight mixture, such as peat or coir, it is helpful if as much of the potting medium as possible is removed and the roots spread out in the planting hole. This helps get over the problem some plants have in transferring from an artificially soft compost to the real world of soil.

CONTAINERS

Containers offer exciting and creative possibilities but also present various problems; plants are vulnerable to drying out and to extremes of temperature. Pots for tall plants need to be heavy, and the mixture should be soil-based or have gravel added to weight the plant down to prevent it blowing over. Slow-release fertilizer granules are a good annual addition to soil, since they save time-consuming liquid feeding throughout summer.

All containers, apart from those used for bog plants, should have holes in the bottom to allow for drainage. Remember that by giving the plants more root room, you are encouraging them to grow, which space may not allow. Consider additional feeding to maintain them at their current size. instead of potting on—palms are surprisingly happy in small pots.

Watering should be regular, even daily in summer. It is crucial to the health and appearance of many plants; large-leaved perennials and bamboos are moisture-lovers and will suffer if they dry out. Such plants should not have their pots exposed to the full sun in summer, as the roots like to be cool as well as moist. Roots are also exposed to cold in winter and are more likely to suffer frost damage. Avoid this by wrapping containers in several layers of bubble plastic, with perhaps another layer over the top of the soil.

Do not combine permanent and temporary plantings in the same container; plants may compete to each other's detriment, and digging in of seasonal plants will cause root damage to the permanent denizens.

MAINTENANCE

Bold and exotic plants do not need much maintaining. In fact, a lot of "maintenance" has more to do with our expectations of neatness than the needs of the plants.

CLEARING DEAD GROWTH

Perennials produce a lot of dead growth every autumn which at some stage needs to be cleared away, to be composted or shredded and returned to the soil as mulch. Traditionally, this task was carried out in the autumn. However, given that the dead seed heads of many bold perennials are a dramatic winter sight, this is best held off until late winter. Leaving them this late also provides a source of food for birds and helps in the identification process if you do any replanting.

MULCHING

Mulching—covering the surface of the ground with an inert layer of material that is usually organic in origin—reduces water loss by evaporation and can dramatically reduce the incursion of weed seeds. Ideally, the plants should mesh together for most of the growing season to cover the ground anyway, which serves the same purpose. Nevertheless, mulching is a major boon in the low-maintenance garden and is an especial help to woody plants, which are often slow to establish, and moisture-lovers growing in less-than-moist conditions.

If gravel is used rather than organic matter, allow some to show through beneath the foliage, as it is an ornamental as much as a functional mulch.

PRUNING

No bold or exotic plant needs pruning, unless you are going to indulge in topiary, which is another book! Some will need tidying up, though, if they are to always look their best. For example, the old canes on bamboos can be removed to allow the fresher, and often more colorful, young canes to shine through.

Regular pruning will be vital, though, if you want to grow plants whose eventual size will be too big for the space allocated. On page 73 we saw how trees can be pruned every few years to restrict their size and enhance leaf size. Vigorous climbers may need to have side shoots cut back to the main stem every year, too, once established. And some bold-leaved shrubs may benefit from training if they are to fit into a tight space. Figs (*Ficus carica*), for example, are sometimes grown as an espalier against a warm wall, where the stems are tied to training wires and any projecting twigs cut back, resulting in a plant that hugs the wall. In theory, this can be done to any well-branched shrubs, but in practice there are few bold shrubs that fit into this category.

TYING IN AND TRAINING CLIMBERS

All bold climbers need supports for them to cling to, unless they are being trained into a tree, in which case the lead shoots should be tied by twine up to a low-growing branch and then left to get on with it.

Wires held horizontally, or vertically, between vine-eyes is the usual support for a climber on a wall or a fence. This is relatively cheap, flexible, quick to do, and if done properly, secure. Trellis is another alternative, and if large expanses are attached to a wall, a considerable area can be covered. It is more expensive and a more time-consuming job than using wire, though.

Climbers will initially need tying into their supports, and occasional inspections should be made to make sure the stems have not outgrown their ties and that no great long shoots are waving around aimlessly in mid-air. Large loops of shoot that mature in a position where they stick out unsupported can look very messy and even create structural problems for the plant.

BELOW: A young *Ricinus communis*, or castor oil plant, in a pot looks forward to being transplanted to its final position and spreading out its vast bronzed leaves. An annual, it can be raised from seed sown under glass with some added bottom heat, such as in a propagator.

OPPOSITE: Hostas are clump-formers by habit and so are very easy to propagate by division: one mature clump can produce as many as five or six smaller plants. But remember that too many hostas planted together can be monotonous—the filigree foliage of ferns would make a good contrast.

PROPAGATION

Of all categories of plant, bold and exotic plants offer some of the greatest problems in propagating. With shrubs it is because of the large-leaved habit that tends to make them so distinctive, along with the limited number of branches produced. Shoots used as cuttings rarely root as readily as small-leaved ones, and species with few shoots offer little cutting material anyway. Big perennials tend to bulk up slowly, again offering few shoots to divide. It is only recent advances in micro-propagation science that have allowed some bold and exotic plants to be marketed at all widely anyway.

In practice, many of the these plants that are slow or difficult to propagate are not the kind of thing that amateur gardeners want many of anyway. Who would want to mass propagate the giant rhubarb *Gunnera manicata*? Smaller plants tend not to be so problematic. As cuttings have little role in propagating relatively few of these plants, we will discuss only division and seed.

DIVISION

This is the standard method for dividing perennials. Clumps of plants are split, either by hand or by working in two garden forks back to back and levering them apart. Most perennials can be divided when they are dormant, but if you are feeling cautious, wait until early spring, when warm weather will mean more rapid root growth. Divided clumps, unless very small, can be treated as new plants and put straight out into their final planting places. Grasses and bamboos should not be split until late spring or early summer, however, when the divisions should be kept shaded and watered in a nursery bed if a hot summer is expected, waiting to be planted out in their final positions in the autumn.

Most of the clump-forming bold perennials will have developed enough shoots within three to five years after planting to produce at least a few new plants, although the slower kinds will look better for not being divided quite as soon as this.

SEED

This is a valuable, and indeed often the only, way of propagating plants from which cuttings are rarely successful or which do not have the kind of clumping growth that makes division worthwhile. It also means many new plants can be raised. The seed of many plants, woody ones especially, is often very slow to germinate, and may need to go through a cycle of warming and chilling that replicates seasonal temperature change before there is germination. All fruit in berries should have the flesh washed off thoroughly before sowing, as it may contain germination inhibitors. The seed should be sown in pans of suitable sterile medium, covered in ¼–½ inch of grit to discourage moss, and then sealed in plastic bags and kept in light shade. It is best sown as soon as it is ripe, that is, in autumn. If you are lucky, it will come up in spring, if not maybe later in the summer, or not until the next spring.

Once the seedlings are large enough to handle, they should be pricked out into small pots or a slug-free, weed-free nursery bed and grown on until they are large enough to go into their permanent positions.

SUPPLIERS

KURT BLUEMEL INC.

2740 Greene Lane
Baldwin
MD 21013
tel: 800 248 PLUG (7584)
fax: 410 557 9785
website: www.bluemel.com

*Grasses, perennials, native plants,
bamboo, ferns, sedges, and exotics.
Outlets across the U.S.*

**DAYDREAMER AQUATIC AND
PERENNIAL GARDENS**

Route 1, Box 438
Belpre
OH 45714
tel: 740 423 4729
website:
www.daydreamergardens.com

Water and bogside plants a specialty

FANCY FRONDS

P.O. Box 1090
Gold Bar
WA 98251
tel: 360 793 1472

Fine foliage plants

FORESTFARM NURSERY

990 Tetherow Road
Williams
OR 97544
tel: 541 846 7269
website: www.forestfarm.com

*Grasses, perennials, bamboos,
ornamentals, ferns, and groundcover
plants*

HERONSWOOD NURSERY

7530 N.E. 288th Street
Kingston
WA 98346
tel: 360 297 4172
website: www.heronswood.com

*Wide selection of shrubs, trees, vines,
grasses, perennials, and "temperennials"
—unusual tender plants*

HICKORY MOUNTAIN PLANT FARM

148 Hadley Mill Road
Pittsboro
NC 27312
tel: 919 542 0360
website: www.hostafarm.com

*Wide range of hostas and shade-loving
perennials*

MORNING GLORY FARM

P.O. Box 423
Fairview
TN 37062
tel: 615 799 0138
fax: 615 799 8864
e-mail: staff@morninggloryfarm.com
website: www.morninggloryfarm.com

Annuals, ferns, grasses, perennials

PLANT DELIGHTS NURSERY

9241 Sauls Road
Raleigh
NC 27603
tel: 919 772 4792
fax: 919 662 0370
e-mail: office@plantdel.com
website: www.plant.del.com

Unusual foliage plants

PRAIRE RESTORATIONS INC.

Prairie Creak Farm
P.O. Box 305
Cannon Falls
MN 55009
tel: 507 663 1091
fax: 507 663 1228
website: www.prairieresto.com

*Seeds and plants of native grasses and
wildflowers*

SISKIYOU RARE PLANTS NURSERY

Department W
2825 Cummings Road
Medford
OR 97501
tel: 541 772 6846
fax: 541 772 4917
e-mail: srgn@wave.net
website: www.wave.net/ugn/srgn

Unusual shrubs and perennials

STAR GARDENS

6409 Burns 307
Austin
TX 78782
tel: 512 454 8714
e-mail: stargardens@hotmail.com

Exotics, ornamentals, perennials, ferns

TRIPPLE BROOK FARM

37 Middle Road
Southampton
MA 01073
tel: 413 527 4626
fax: 413 527 9853
website: www.tripplebrookfarm.com

*Over 300 species of native plants, cold-
hardy exotics, perennials, bamboos,
grasses, ferns*

TWOMBLY NURSERY

163 Barn Hill Road
Monroe
CT 06468
tel: 203 261 2133
fax: 203 261 9230
e-mail: info@twomblynursery.com
website: www.unusualplants.com

Hard-to-find and unusual plants

WE-DU NURSERIES

Route 5, Box 724
Marion
NC 28752
tel: 704 738 8300
website: www.we-du.com

*Rhododendrons, grasses, ferns, trees,
and shrubs*

WOODLANDERS

1128 Colleton Avenue
Aiken
SC 29801
tel: 803 648 7522

Foliage plants

INDEX

Entries in **bold** refer to the Directory pages 74–95. Entries in *italics* refer to captions.

A

Acanthus species 45, 55; *mollis* Latifolius group **76**, *76*
Actinidia: chinensis 61; *deliciosa* 21, 50, **76**, *76–7;* 'Hayward' *105*
Aesculus species 30, **76;** *angustifolia* 76
Agave species 17, 55, *55, 66,* **76–7**, *77,* 101; *americana* 'Variegata' *22, 71, 75*
Ailanthus altissima **77**
Allium species *24–5*
Aloe species 17, 55, *66,* **77;** *plicatilis* 77
Amaranthus varieties 37
Angelica species 18, 49, **77;** *archangelica* *47, 48; atropurpurea* 48
annuals 37, *37–8,* 62, 65, *66, 66*
Aralia species 30, 50, **77;** *elata* 18, *42, 43,* 77
Araucaria araucana 18, *28,* 43, **78**
Arisaema species 52; *serratum 78;* *triphyllum* 78
Aristolochia: kaempferi 104; macro *-phylla 8,* 21, *48,* 50, **78**, *78*
Aruncus dioicus 52, 53, **78**, *78*
Arundo donax 58, 61, *72–3,* **78–9;** 'Variegata' *78;* 'Versicolor' *58,* 65
Asphodeline lutea 23, 55
Asplenium scolopendrium 52, *74,* **79**
Astilboides tabularis 13, 20, **79**

B

bamboo species 24, 26, 30, 43, 44, 53, *60–1,* 66, 69, *71, 72–3,* 73, *98–101,* *106 see also Arundinaria; Chusquea;* *Fargesia; Petasites; Semiarundinaria*

banana species 61; ornamental *see* *Ensete;* true *see Musa*
bear's breeches *see Acanthus*
bedding schemes *37–8,* 62, *64–5,* 65
Bergenia 48, 66, *79, 79*
Blechnum chilense 8, 53, **79**, *79*
blue pine *see Pinus wallichiana*
bog plants 20, *56–8, 58–9,* 59, 102
border plantings *46–7, 46–7,* 66
buckeye *see Aesculus*
burnet *see Sanguisorba*

C

Calamagrostis x *acutiflora* 'Karl Foerster' *25,* **79**
Canna hybrids *10,* 36, 37, *37, 41,* 61, *61, 62, 64,* **80**, *80,* 101; *iridiflora* 37
cardoon *see Cynara cardunculus*
Carex: morrowii 'Variegata' *34; pendula* *24,* 34, **80**, 81
Carpinus betulus 'Fastigiata' 30
castor oil plant *see Ricinus communis*
Catalpa bignonioides 13, 30, *30–1,* **80**, *81;* 'Aurea' *17*
Cedrus libani subsp. *atlantica* 'Glauca' *34*
Chamaedorea 38
Chamaerops humilis 22, 23, 43, 55
Chinese gooseberry *see Actinidia* *deliciosa*
Chusan palm *see Trachycarpus fortunei*
Chusquea culeou 30, 43, 73, **80**, *81*
Clematis armandii 61, *68–9,* **80–1**
clary sage *see Salvia sclarea*
climbers 21, *21,* 50, 61, *68–9,* 69, 73, *105*
color *24–5, 26, 28, 29,* 48, 50, 51, 62, 66
combination plantings *44–5, 44–5*
conifers 30, 66
containers 17, *17,* 44, 66, *66–7,* 69, 70, *71,* 73, 101, 102
Cordyline species 13, *16,* 17, *17, 22,* 38, 61, 62, 66, 70, 101; *australis* 17, *54,* 69, **81**, *81*

Cornus controversa 30, 43, **81**
Cortaderia selloana 18, 34, 45, **81;** 'Rendatleri' *34,* 43, *43*
courtyards 43, *68–9, 68–9*
Crambe cordifolia 12, 55, 70, **82**, *82*
Crocosmia species 23; 'Lucifer' *47, 62,* 82, *82*
Cupressus sempervirens 24, 55, 82
Cynara cardunculus 11, 12, 18, *19,* 50, 65, **82**, *82*
Cyperus eragrostis 51
cypresses 29; Italian *see Cupressus* *sempervirens*

D

date palm *see Phoenix*
Darmera peltata 12, 20, *20, 56–8,* 57, **82**, *82–3*
daylilies 46; *see also Hemerocallis*
devil's walking stick *see Aralia elata*
Dicentra 'Stuart Boothman' *53*
Dicksonia antarctica 13, *58–9,* *60–1,* 61, **83**
Dipsacus fullonum 51
doublefile viburnum *see Viburnum* *plicatum* 'Mariesii'
Dracaena 38, 62
dry places 54, 55, *55,* 70, 71
Dryopteris species 52, *53; dilatata 12,* **83**
Dutchman's pipe *see Aristolochia*
dwarf fan palm *see Chamaerops humilis*

E

Echinops 33; *ritro 10,* 33
elephant's ears *see Bergenia*
empress tree *see Paulownia tomontosa*
Ensete ventricosum 37
Eremurus 24, *25,* 33
Eryngium species 23, 55, **83;** *agavifolium 23; bourgatii 23;* *giganteum 10,* **83**

eucalyptus **83**, *83*
Eupatorium purpureum subsp.
  maculatum 33
Euphorbia species 55; *amygdaloides 48;*
  characias 48; lathyris **84;** *mellifera* 26,
  26, 48, 61, 69, 84, *84,* 98
European seakale *see Crambe cordifolia*
evergreens 26, *26, 28,* 29, 34, 43, 46,
  48, *48,* 52, *52–3,* 53, 66, *68,* 69
exotics 38, 60–1, *60–1*

F

fan palm *see Chamaerops humilis*
Fargesia mureliae **84**
Fascicularia pitcairnifolia 14, **84,** *85*
x *Fatshedera lizei* **84**
Fatsia japonica 18, 21, 30, 43, 53, 65,
  66, 69, *69,* 70, **84,** *85,* 98–101
feather reed grass *see Calamagrostis* x
  acutiflora 'Karl Foerster'
ferns 26, *27,* 52, *52–3,* 58–9, 69
Ferula communis **84,** *85*
Ficus carica 8, 21, *73,* **84**
fig species 38 *see also Ficus*
focal points *16–17, 17,* 44, 62
foliage 10, *12,* 13, 20–1, *20–1,* 21, 24,
  24, 25, 26, *26–7,* 29, 46, 38, 47, 48,
  55, *59, 61, 73, 78, 99 see also* spikes
  and rosettes
foxgloves 46 *see also Digitalis*
foxtail lilies *see Eremurus*

G

garlics, ornamental *see Allium*
giant dogwood *see Cornus controversa*
giant hogweed *see Heracleum*
  mantegazzanium
giant reed *see Arundo donax*
grasses 24, 25, *25,* 34, *34–5,* 37, 43, *43,*
  46, *58–9,* 66, 106
Griselinia littoralis 26, **85,** *85,* 101;
  'Variegata' 16
Gunnera species 20, 33, 70, 101;
  manicata 10, 20, *32–3,* 48, 56, *56,*
  73, **85,** *85; tinctoria* 56, 73

H

half-hardy plants *36, 37,* 37–8, 38–9;
  managing 101
hart's tongue fern *see Asplenium*
  scolopendrium
Hedera: canariensis 52, *53,* 69, **85;** *helix*
  52; *Hedychium gardnerianum* **86**
Helianthus annuus 37
Helleborus species 32, 66; *argutifolius*
  32, **86;** *foetidus* 26, 32, 52, **86,** *86*
Heracleum: lehmanniaum 10, 18;
  mantegazzanium 10, 18, 43, 51, **86,**
  86
Himalayan white pine *see Pinus*
  wallichiana
holly 30, *41,* 66
honey spurge *see Euphorbia mellifera*
honey bush *see Melianthus major*
hornbeam *see Carpinus*
horse chestnut *see Aesculus*
Hosta species 17, 33, 52, 69, 66, 73,
  107; *elata* 52; *sieboldiana 17, 32–3,*
  33, *52,* 87; var. 'Elegans' **86**
Hydrangea species 30; *aspera 8,* 21, 50,
  50, 53; 'Macrophylla' 13; Villosa
  Group **87;** *quercifolia 30,* 51, **87,** *87*

I

Indian bean tree *see Catalpa bignonoides*
Indocalamus latifolius **87**

indumentum 21
invasive plants 58, *58–9,* 73
Iris species 23, 24, *24–5,* 46;
  foetidissima 29, **87;** *japonica* 87, *87;*
  pseudoacorus 59; 'Variegata' 59
ivy species 52, 69; *see also Hedera*

J

Jacob's rod *see Asphodeline lutea*
Japanese angelica tree *see Aralia elata*
Japanese vine *see Vitis coignetiae*
Japanese aralia *see Fatsia japonica* 73
Japanese sedge *see Carex morrowii*
Juniperus: communis 'Hibernica' 55;
  scopulorum 'Skyrocket' 24, 55, **87**

K

Kalopanax septemlobus **88**
Kirengeshoma palmata 32–3
kiwi fruit *see Actinidia deliciosa*
Kniphofia species 23, 24, 46, 55, **88,** *88;*
  caulescens **88**

L

Lavandula species 55
leatherleaf viburnum *see Viburnum*
  rhytidophyllum
leaves *see* foliage
Levisticum officinale 48, **88**
Ligularia species 50, 53, 57, 70, **88;**

ACKNOWLEDGMENTS

THE AUTHOR would like to thank Andrea Jones for her work in photographing the plants for this book, Susan Berger for her help with the directory, and the owners of all the gardens featured.

THE PHOTOGRAPHER would like to thank Russell Sharp and Phillip Brown at the Gardens of Portmeirion, North Wales; Lin Randall of the Savill Garden, Windsor Great Park; Angus White of Architectural Plants; Fergus Garrett, head gardener of Great Dixter, for his help and Christopher Lloyd for his permission to photograph; Paul and Diana Whittaker from P.W. Plants for their help and hospitaility; Simon Trehane of Trehane Gardens; Marion Holder; Mr. and Mrs. Stoner; Jason Payne, garden designer; Claudia Beurer and Gerald Singel of Gruga Park Botanic Gardens; M. E Berthelot and M. M. Couzet of La Bambouserie; Alan Bloom of Blooms of Bressingham; John Nelson, Tim Smit and the staff at the Lost Gardens of Heligan; Sue and Bleddyn Wynn-Jones; Hugh Angus, Tony Russell and Peter Gregory of Westonbirt Arboretum; Mr. and Mrs. Henry Bungener; Mr. and Mrs. John Lenting; Greg Redwood of the Garden Developments Unit, Royal Botanic Gardens, Kew; Dr. and Mrs. Marsden of Garwell House; Beth Chatto.

PICTURE CREDITS

l = left   r = right   t = top   b = bottom   c = center

Apple Court p79 No.5; **Architectural Plants** p28b, p51cr, p53bl, p54, pp60-61t, p76 No.2, p78 No.4, p102; **Blooms of Bressingham** p99; **Beth Chatto's Garden** pp23-24b, p44t, p78 No.2; **La Bambouserie** p24tl, p51b, p60tr, p97; **Cowley Manor** p57b, pp72-73; **Crûg Farm** p6, pp32-33t, p52c, p78 No.1, p104, p107; **Garwell House** p43t, p89 No.6, p92 No.3; **Great Dixter** p10tl, p18tr, p18bl, p21tl, p36, p39, p46t&b, p47t, p56t, p62tl, p63, p65 t&b, p95 No.6; **Gruga Park** p23t&b, p24t, p31, p42, p45tr, p51tr, p81 No.3, p88 No.3, p91 Nos 2&3, p94 No.3, p106; **Gillian Harris** p 10tr&bl, p62tr, p66bl; **Lost Gardens of Heligan** p8bl, p13tr, p16, p18b, p22t, p58br, p89 No.4, p98; **Hermanshof, near Weinheim, Germany** p24tr, p33br, p34b, p44b, p46c, p52tr, p78 No.3, p93 No.7, p94 No.1; **Marion Holder** p68 all pics; **Japanese Garden and Bonsai Nursery** p58cr, p59tr, p81 No.2; **Lady Farm, Avon** p35; **Lamorran House, St. Mawes, Cornwall** p14, p60b, p68-69, p85 No. 2; **Old Vicarage, East Rushton, Norfolk** p12br, p17t, p19, p29, p30 b, p37, p38t, p41, p50t, p64, p66 t&br, p67, p73t; **Piet Oudolf, Holland** p40, p45c, p51tl, p94 No.2; **Jason Payne** p72 all pics; **P.W. Plants** p52b; **Rowden Gardens** p 11, p48tr, p53r, p56b, p57tl&tr, p59tl, p96; **Royal Botanic Gardens, Kew** p30t, p55b, p76 No.3, p77 No.5, p81 No.4, p83 No.5, p85 No.4; **Savill Garden** p27, p82 No.2; **Speckhardt** p12bl, p53cl; **Stoners** p71tr&bl; **Trehane** p53tl, p74, p90 No.1, p93 No.5; **Mr. Way, Winchester** p13bl, p17bl, p38b, p69, p71tl, p100; **Westenbirt Arboretum** p12tr; **Patrick Wyniatt-Hussey (Regent's Park Flower Show)** p70, p71br.

ZONE 1	-Below -50°F
ZONE 2	-50 to -40°F
ZONE 3	-40° to -30°F
ZONE 4	-30° to -20°F
ZONE 5	-20° to -10°F
ZONE 6	-10° to 0°F
ZONE 7	+0° to 10°F
ZONE 8	+10° to 20°F
ZONE 9	+20° to 30°F
ZONE 10	+30° to 40°F
ZONE 11	+Above 40°F

11
11